More Praise for
SALTWATER BUDDHA

"A motivating book that reminds us to follow our hearts without fear and limitations. Refreshing, easy-to-read, and a lot of fun."—Urijah Faber

"In this terrific first book, Jaimal Yogis has done what every artist and writer strives to do: he has made something beautiful and universal from the particulars of his own life. *Saltwater Buddha* will surely find the audience it deserves—among surfers, among seekers, and among those who enjoy being swept along on a curious ride."—**Daniel Duane, author of *Caught Inside***

"Jaimal Yogis starts off as an Everyteen with two deep hungers— to learn surfing and to calm his mind—and his simple, amused, deadly serious report on how he tries to satisfy those desires may ultimately launch an entirely new breed of memoir: the coming-of-sage story. Yogis's prose is etched yet effortless, a conversation with a friend who pretends to be naïve, but has clearly drunk up so much life experience that you trust his authority as a truth-teller more than you know. He rocked me happily for chapters as he recounted his journey from an Atlantic island to California suburbs to a series of beach towns (including, memorably, Brooklyn). But each time I was lulled, I always was also on edge, wondering if bigger surf may be coming. Indeed, it was: several moving, sharp-edged episodes—sets, really—that will stay vivid in my mind for a long, long time."—**Bruce Kelley, editor-in-chief of *San Francisco* Magazine**

"At sixteen, Jaimal Yogis ran away on a spiritual journey of a magnitude few of us even dream of, to learn to ride the waves of the world's oceans, and the bigger surf within his own mind. As Jaimal gains hard-won spiritual lessons with a teenager's eagerness and a surfer's passion, we cannot help but see our own spiritual life with fresh, beginner's eyes. His journey started in nothingness—at least in a material sense. But it ends in deep riches of spiritual insight, human warmth, and humor. The pages kept turning. I couldn't put this book down."—**Michael Ellsberg, coauthor of *Flirting with Disaster***

SALTWATER BUDDHA

SALTWATER BUDDHA

A SURFER'S QUEST TO
FIND ZEN ON THE SEA

JAIMAL YOGIS

Wisdom Publications • Boston

Wisdom Publications
199 Elm Street
Somerville MA 02144 USA
www.wisdompubs.org

Library of Congress Cataloging-in-Publication Data
Yogis, Jaimal.
 Saltwater Buddha : a surfer's quest to find Zen on the sea / by Jaimal
Yogis.
    p. cm.
 ISBN 0-86171-535-7 (pbk. : alk. paper)
1. Yogis, Jaimal. 2. Buddhists—Biography. 3. Surfing—Religious
aspects—Buddhism. 4. Buddhism. I. Title.

 BQ998.O43A3 2009
 294.3'927092—dc22
 [B]

                              2008054063

13 12 11 10 09
 5 4 3 2 1

Cover design by Phil Pascuzzo. Interior design by Tony Lulek. Set in Sabon
11/15.

Wisdom Publications' books are printed on acid-free paper and meet the
guidelines for permanence and durability of the Production Guidelines for
Book Longevity of the Council on Library Resources.

Printed in the United States of America.

Excerpts by Hung-chih on pages 1 and 226 are from Nelson Foster and Jack
Schoemaker, eds., *The Roaring Stream: A New Zen Reader* (Hopewell NJ:
The Ecco Press, 1996), 178. Excerpt by Hung-chih on page 63 is from Taigen
Dan Leighton, *Cultivating the Empty Field: The Silent Illumination of Zen
Master Hongzhi* (Boston: Tuttle Publishing, 2000), 24.

Table of Contents

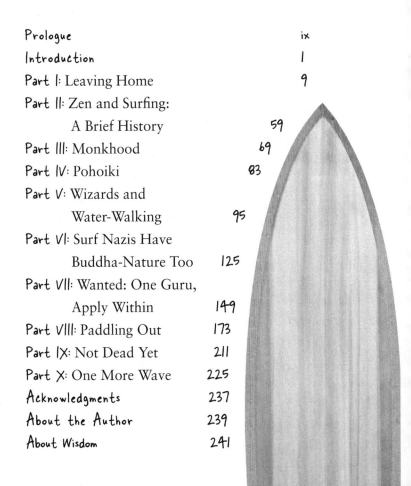

Prologue

The ocean is in constant flux, and when you spend a lot of time in it you become like a floating bottle with a message inside; you know you're going somewhere, sense you have a purpose, but you also know you're at the mercy of the winds and currents, that surrendering may be your only good option.

Lately I've been surfing a lot. And there's something different about the saltwater life. One becomes floppy, like seaweed, while at the same time agile, like an eel. One becomes, I suppose, more like water itself. The *Tao Te Ching* says, "Nothing in the world is more flexible and yielding than water. Yet when it attacks the firm and the strong, none can withstand it. They have no way to change it."

This is a book in praise of water. On its surface, it is a series of short stories about my encounters with the sea and Zen practice. But underneath, it's just a homily about water—to that which sustains life.

I am no expert on Zen, and certainly no expert surfer. But I have an ongoing love affair with the ocean, which, through years of meditation, I have come to view through what might be called Zen-colored glasses. If I have a message inside this empty vessel— if it hasn't been completely dissolved by the saltwater leaking in—this book is it. May the winds blow it to shores where it will be useful.

Introduction

In water, everything is "dissolved."
—Mircea Eliade

A person of the Way fundamentally does not dwell anywhere. The white clouds are fascinated with the green mountain's foundation. The bright moon cherishes being carried along with the flowing water.
—Hung-chih

Ua ka ua, kahe ka wai.
The rain rains, the water flows.
—Hawaiian Proverb

In Zen there is nothing to explain, nothing to teach that will add to your knowledge. Unless it grows out of yourself, no knowledge is really of value to you, a borrowed plumage never grows.
—D.T. Suzuki

wo weeks ago, I moved onto my girlfriend's dad's sailboat in Sausalito. *Dulce* is the boat's name. She is thirty feet long, mostly white with lacquered wooden paneling around the windows. Her sails are wrapped in teal canvas.

At first, I thought *Dulce* rocked too much. But now she lulls me to sleep. The bed is so small, curling up in it while the waves lap against the hull is a bit like returning to the womb: not that I remember the womb, of course, but I imagine it to be something like sleeping in the bow of a sailboat.

I don't sail. Simply to live on the water is the point. After a couple years sequestered inland, always driving to the coast for surf, being on the boat feels like a homecoming. "To come back down to the ocean," writes Thomas Farber, in *On Water*, "is to reexperience an essential memory trace, something once known well, to recall that one has been trying to remember." I like that Farber writes "to recall *that* one has been trying to remember" rather than, "to recall *what* one has been trying to remember." It describes the truth that when away from the sea you can easily forget what you feel homesick for. But the vestiges are always there. And upon return, the salt air, the incessant roar of waves, what Mark Twain calls the "limpid depths."

Basho, the seventeenth-century Zen monk and poet, said in a haiku:

INTRODUCTION

Mother I never knew
Every time I see the ocean
Every time

Maybe having evolved from aqueous amoebas, and being in our current form two-thirds water, we are hardwired to connect to the sea.

Or maybe we are even part of water's big plan. Tom Robbins suggests that human beings (like every other living creature) "were invented by water as a device for transporting itself from one place to another."

Farber points out that we are not so far removed from the sea as we think: our skin is smooth like that of a dolphin or whale; our fingers and toes are slightly webbed; we float; we are streamlined and surrounded with a subcutaneous layer of fat; our blood itself is close to the consistency of seawater. And as demonstrated in recent years by free divers, we even have the capability, like dolphins and whales, to slow down our heart rate in order to reach great depths—more than 400 feet without oxygen.

THE VIEW FROM THE BOAT is impressionistic: specks of light flickering on the bay like stars looking up. The golden grasses of Angel Island twitch under the first rays of light. Directly south, the San Francisco skyline stretches up, barely cresting a comforter of fog—"a city inside a snow globe," as Anne Lamott once described it. North, Mount Tamalpais, a pyramid of green, blocks the winds, creates this sanctuary: one of the most expensive stretches of waterfront property on the planet—expensive, that is, unless you live on your girlfriend's dad's sailboat.

As on many mornings in Marin, there is this sly strip of fog—water in its most mystical incarnation—slithering over, around, and through the hills, making everything look ancient and unsolved. I climb back down into the cabin, a cramped space barely tall enough for me to stand in, and sit down on a little bench, pulling my legs into full lotus: left foot on right thigh, right foot on left. Today will begin, as most mornings do, with a little zazen, a little Zen meditation.

It's such a common word these days, Zen, used mostly it seems for marketing, as in the current ad campaign for MP3 players—"*Find Your Zen*"—or San Francisco restaurants—*Hana Zen, Now and Zen*. But many people have no idea what real Zen is. And sometimes I fear I don't, either. I know what the word means, of course. Literally, *Zen* is Japanese for a Sanskrit term, *dhyana*, that translates loosely as "meditation." *Dhyana*, as I have heard it described by one of my most academically versed meditation teachers, might better be translated as "the concentration that is completed," a focus that encompasses rather than narrows.

INTRODUCTION

The Zen school of Buddhism arose in China around the fourth century CE when a South Indian Buddhist monk named Bodhidharma allegedly brought the "mind-only" teaching there and started a lineage. The tradition's simplicity, rigor, and wit flourished and eventually spread through much of Asia, becoming well known to Americans only in this past century.

But Zen is more than a lineage, more than a practice of sitting still. It's more than an aesthetic style, and certainly more than a marketing scheme. It is an attempt to express the ineffable, the deepest paradox of being. And its definition alone may be as indescribable as its core teaching. One of the great pioneers of Zen in America, Shunryu Suzuki Roshi, often said Zen is best expressed simply by sitting.

In my limited experience, Zen practice has been something like returning to the waterfront, or like paddling out into the surf after days without waves. Matthieu Ricard, the French biologist who ordained under the Dalai Lama, writes of the stages of meditation: "Finally, the mind becomes like the sea in calm weather. Ripples of discursive thoughts occasionally run over its surface, but in the depths, it is never disturbed." Sitting quietly in zazen or on my surfboard, I am reminded that I've somehow been away from myself too long, that I need to return more often.

It makes sense to me that surfing and Buddhism should meet in a concrete form, a book. "Surfing is really more than anything else a faith," says former editor of *Surfer* magazine Sam George. And surfers often sound like Buddhists in describing their art. "Then the world vanished," writes Steven Kotler in his surfing memoir *West of Jesus*. "There was no self, no other. For an instant, I didn't know where I ended and the wave began." The photograph of pro surfers Dick Brewer, Gerry Lopez, and Reno Abellira meditating cross-legged next to their surfboards at Mount Tantalus has been branded into the mind of almost every surfer. More recently, meditating pro surfer Dave Rastovich ("Rasta") has become something of a guardian angel to the sport, instructing other surfers in forms of meditation and helping rescue dolphins and whales in his spare time.

On the other side of the spectrum, Buddhist teachers have often employed water metaphors to express the Buddha's teachings: impermanence ("The myriad worlds are like so much foam on the sea," wrote eighth-century Chinese master Yung-Chia), karma and reincarnation (a human's life force will "produce the next life just as the energy of one wave produces the next wave. This energy will never disappear, resulting in a continuous formation of successive lives," according to the twentieth-century master Hakuun Yasutani), and the fundamental buddha-nature within everyone (it "is like the sea, and each individual is like a wave on the surface of the ocean," says Yasutani).

But my all-time favorite Zen-surfing quote is by Suzuki Roshi, one of the people credited with helping to bring Zen to America, via—where else?—California. Suzuki founded Tassajara Zen Center in Big Sur (near some of the best surf on the West Coast) and I like to think he had surfers in mind when comparing thought waves to ocean waves. He said, "Even though waves arise, the essence of mind is pure... Waves are the practice of water. To speak of waves apart from water or water apart from waves is a delusion."

Yes: enough talk of tepid, serene pools reflecting moonlight. Let us speak of waves, of glassy ocean surfaces enlivened with surging swells. If waves are the practice of water, and thoughts the practice of mind, wouldn't it be wonderful if we all learned to surf?

SOME SAY THAT THE "GOAL" OF BUDDHISM is to become a Buddha—to become awake. And one of the historical Buddha's very first teachings, recorded in the *Avatamsaka Sutra*, says "the Earth expounds Dharma," meaning, I think, that the very world we live in describes how to awaken. And since most of the earth is ocean, I don't think it's going too far to say that, with the right intention and awareness, you can learn to be a Buddha by playing in the waves.

My parents introduced me to Buddhism. But I fell in love with it in high school through the Beats. I recall reading Kerouac's *Dharma Bums* and almost weeping with joy when Japhy (modeled on the Beat poet Gary Snyder) tells Jack, "I meet my bodhisattvas on the street." I could hardly fathom a religious tradition in which I could find truth wherever I go, on my own. I soon found out the historical Buddha stressed that I *had to* find it on my own. I could get help from the Triple Jewels, of course: the Buddha, the Dharma (the teachings), and the Sangha (the community of practitioners). But ultimately, the Buddha said to test everything on your own, make your own proof.

Upon his deathbed, the Buddha spoke these final words: "All things are impermanent. Work out your own salvation with diligence."

Ridiculous as it may be, I see myself doing just that as I flail around on the sea, gliding on the fringes of our blue world.

Part I
LEAVING HOME

While still young, a black-haired young man endowed with the blessing of youth, in the prime of life, though my mother and father wished otherwise and wept with tearful faces, I shaved off my hair and beard, put on the ochre robe, and went forth from the home life into homelessness.

—The Buddha

Indeed, one feels microscopically small, and the thought that one may wrestle with this sea raises in one's imagination a thrill of apprehension, almost fear. Why, they are a mile long, these bull-mouthed monsters, and they weigh a thousand tons, and they charge into shore faster than a man can run. What chance? No chance at all, is the verdict of the shrinking ego.

—Jack London,
writing of waves and his first surf session

1. WHEN I WAS THREE, my dad got stationed at a U.S. airbase on the island of Terceira off the coast of Portugal. We flew there on a military cargo jet, ears plugged to soften the engine roar. We moved into a white adobe apartment above a shoe store where wool-sweatered men smoked cigars and stray dogs begged.

This was before my parents started fighting and years before their divorce, so there were four of us in the family. A round number, I often thought, a good number.

My older sister, Ciel, and I found endless satisfaction in the novelties of the island: the bullfights on cobblestone streets, the patchwork lava rock walls that quilted the hills, the serrated bluffs dotted with old fishermen, the spitting llamas. We adopted fourteen puppies and fed them oatmeal. We built forts out of mud. We climbed into the foggy hills and searched for wizards. Most of all, we loved the beach.

The *praia*—as we called it in an attempt to feel local—lay just down the street, a two-minute walk. We could always hear it and smell it. The beach was littered with trash; the wall at its border was stained in graffiti and urine. But the sand was soft and the ocean warmed by the Gulf Stream.

My dad taught us to body-surf. As a teenager, he'd been a surfer in New York (one of the brazen few who'd surfed Jones Beach in the winter in jeans and a wool sweater) and then in Hawaii while stationed on Oahu during the Vietnam War. He often told us nostalgic tales of big waves, near drowning, heroism. Then he taught us how to watch the waves, how to jump off the sand at just the right moment so the wave caught you in its grip like a baseball mitt and thrust you forward like a roller coaster.

I remember the Atlantic all inky black and rough like crumpled tinfoil. But the inner waves, the ones we rode, were an opaque brownish-green, full of silt and rubbery seaweed. The waves were frightening. But we felt safe with my dad. He could lift us up above the water, or keep us steady in the midst of strong currents.

When a good wave finally came, we laughed and shrieked. Then we turned and dove down the face, shutting our eyes tight, gripping each other's hands.

Sufficiently tumbled, we jogged up to our big yellow blanket where Mom was usually reading a book. We warmed up. And then we talked about the islands together, told stories about their strangeness and magic.

Three years later, my dad got transferred again, this time to McClellan Air Force Base outside Sacramento, two hours from the nearest beach.

It wasn't so bad in the valley. I made new friends. I got a BMX bike and a Variflex skateboard. Mom ran a daycare so there were always screaming kids to play with. Occasionally, the four of us went to the beach near San Francisco and talked about how nice it would be to live by the sea again, if only we could afford it. Maybe someday.

But we never could afford it. My parents divorced after a few years in suburbia. And so there were three of us—a different three every other weekend. Then the numbers of immediate family–members rotated: six, then four, then back to three. But it wasn't weird. It was ordinary. We just grew up: soccer and swim team, keg-stands at the river, fireworks and football. It was a normal American upbringing. I can't complain.

But the sea never left me. I couldn't let go. Or it wouldn't let go. Or both.

2.

> Dear family,
> Please do not worry. I am somewhere in the world and I will call you when I get there. I had some dreams that led me to believe that I need a change and I could not make it here. I'm sorry. I took some money from Mom's credit card and I apologize. I plan to pay it all back when I get settled.
> I love you very much.
>
> Jaimal

BY THE TIME my mom found this note on my bedroom pillow, I was on a one-way flight to Hawaii. I was a junior in high school and had saved a few hundred bucks mowing lawns and selling old baseball cards. Added to the $900 I stole from my mom's credit card (which I did eventually return), I had just enough to start a shiny new life in paradise.

On the ATA flight, movies of waterfalls and women in hula skirts readied us for the islands. And the further from land we flew, the more I felt the shackles of adolescence dissolving. I was reading a book about the Buddha's life, which I knew quite a lot about having grown up with what you might call "New-Agey" parents. (Our home libraries could fill an East-West bookstore.) But I read it again because the Buddha's story made me feel better about running away. I thought of myself as leaving home, much like Prince Siddhartha did, to discover truth.

Siddhartha's story began like this. He was born a prince in present-day Nepal around 2,500 years ago. At his auspicious birth, a soothsayer told his parents that Siddhartha would become a great spiritual teacher and abandon his kingdom, or else he would conquer a vast stretch of land and be a powerful leader. His father wanted the latter, so he tried to shelter his son from the sufferings of the world—old age, sickness, death. He feared exposing the prince to suffering would push him to seek spiritual truth. So the king kept his son surrounded with beauty and youth within the palace and conned him into thinking the whole world was roses and immortality. Of course, Siddhartha, an unusually smart young man, soon realized that it was all a lie, and when he witnessed the real suffering outside the palace—corpses, leprosy, famine, and an ascetic renunciant—he was overwhelmed with compassion and he vowed to do something.

He probably had a hunch suffering arose in the mind and could also cease in the mind. But he wanted to find out for sure. He abandoned the kingdom, renouncing all its pleasures to become a wandering mendicant and focus on ending the suffering within.

LEAVING HOME

I loved Siddhartha's story. And miles above the Pacific, I thought about how similar the prince and I were. My parents, having rejected their native Catholicism and Judaism, had raised Ciel and me to go to Hindu temples, too. Born in my parents' full-fledged hippie phase, I was even named after an Indian saint: Baba Jaimal Singh. And it couldn't have been just coincidence (I thought) that my Lithuanian grandparents' name was shortened to Yogis. I figured I was destined, like Siddhartha, for spiritual greatness.

By running away, all the elements were coming together. I was abandoning the pleasures of the palace. Okay, so I wasn't running away because I was *overwhelmed* with compassion for all living beings, and our four-bedroom home in Sacramento was hardly a palace. But we did have a pool and a hot tub. And I figured that in modern America, most people lived with almost as many luxuries as the prince had 2,500 years ago. And I was giving up quite a bit: television, QUAD 102.5 radio jams, my friends. And just as Siddhartha was fed up with the cycle of birth and death, I was fed up with the endless cycle of suburban trivialities—especially my midnight curfew.

3. BEFORE I COULD CONTINUE living out my version of the Buddha's story, I had to decide which of the seven islands I would settle on. Oahu sounded too Disneyland. The Big Island: too volcanic. I hadn't heard anything about Kauai. I looked for a spiritual sign. The in-flight magazine said that Maui was the "Island of Love." This conjured images of me on the beach with a Hawaiian Tropic model.

I went to Maui.

4. MY PARENTS CALLED THE POLICE:

"Our son ran away," my mom cried.

"Uh-huh," said the officer. "And how do you know this?"

"He left a note."

"Uh-huh. Well, ma'am, we can't pronounce him missing until he's gone a week."

"A week! He could be dead in a week."

"Uh-huh. Well, if it's any consolation, we see this all the time. He says he ran away to some far-off land, but he's probably down the street playing video games at his friend's house."

"He doesn't play video games."

"Uh-huh…"

5. My main goal was to learn to surf. There were, of course, subtexts to this: a struggle for independence; a rebellion against the deadness of suburbia; the first sparks of a spiritual path; a need to shock my parents, especially my dad, from whom I'd grown distant since the divorce.

But surfing trumped all. There had been dreams that needed answers: dreams of waves and surfboards and dolphins and coconuts and breathing underwater and swimming with a fishtail. I awoke from these dreams with a feeling of possibility—more than I could say about life in public high school.

I'd known for some time that I needed to get out of town, away from strip malls and SUVs and especially my friends. I had lots of friends and it's not that they were bad guys. Most of us had grown up together. We all came from nice, middle-class families. We dressed in designer brands crossed with our hardcore skate gear: Think, Plan B, Shorty's. We were popular kids with pretty girlfriends and we went to lots of parties. We drank only the best micro-brews, smoked only the best pot. My friends, all way wealthier than me, drove fancy new cars that we raced through suburban streets like life was something you could order in a catalogue.

I guess maybe it doesn't sound so bad. And I guess it wasn't. But deep down, we were bored. We complained about everything. We wrote ourselves fake parental notes and cut classes and drank ourselves into high-minded stupors. We vandalized things for no particular reason. We lied to our parents constantly because it didn't matter. We acted like everything was okay. But really, I think we felt like the smog that blew in from the coasts and stagnated in the valley. We were stuck.

I always thought life under the valley haze was missing something. I felt too that something got clarified when I went to the coast or up to the snowy peaks. But then I would descend into the haze again— and forget.

I had been in a rebellious phase since the divorce. It began with pyromania (mostly blowing up action figures and Barbie dolls) and concluded with my parents picking me up at a Lake Tahoe police station, drunk and handcuffed to a wooden chair after being arrested for driving drunk.

This, the most recent "big trouble" I'd gotten myself into, began a six-month probation sentence. And my parents reacted as most parents would, withdrawing the only tidbits of freedom I still had, which only made me more restless.

I knew I needed to make changes but didn't feel strong enough around my peers, who all seemed determined to make their lives into a twisted after-school special. So I sought sanctuary in the only thing that still seemed open, malleable, and out of reach of the authorities: my dreams of water.

6. THE MAUI AIRPORT SMELLED OF JASMINE, plumerias, and fresh grass clippings. Don Ho played over the speakers: "tiny bubbles, tiny bubbles, in the wine, in the wine." The air was like silk, no, like rose-water—warm dew.

I collected my bags and giggled, thinking about my new life and freedom. But freedom—I was about to find out—isn't all that fun when you're broke with no car.

I had brought with me these things: a bodyboard, a boom box, a case of CDs, a skateboard, a backpacking pack, a tent, a guitar, a sleeping bag, a skimboard, three pairs of shoes, a duffel bag of clothes, books (Michener's *Hawaii*, *The Teachings of Don Juan*, *The Tao Te Ching*, *The Old Man and the Sea*, *The Dharma Bums*, *Moby Dick*, and *Siddhartha*), and a small metal Buddha statue my dad had brought back from Japan.

After all, I was moving.

Without a car, going anywhere with all this stuff proved impossible. So I bought a mountain bike for $100, which, in fact, made it more impossible. As I pushed my duffel bags on my skateboard and dragged the rest behind me on the pavement, tripping every few steps, the Buddha's teachings—"attachment causes suffering"—started to make literal sense.

But I had enough money to buy *one* cab ride to a nearby campground.

"Traveling alone?" the cabbie asked with a relaxed Hawaiian lounge-singer smile.

"Something like that."

"Best way, brah. Aloooo-ha."

"I hope so."

As night fell, I realized I didn't have food. Or a flashlight. Rain poured down as I assembled the tent, soaking my pile of stuff, which suddenly seemed beyond superfluous. The rain poured harder and the more it poured the more I cried. I bawled. I prayed. The rain washed my salty tears into the sand. The world suddenly seemed very cruel.

And the night was *dark*.

7. THE SUN ROSE EARLY. I awoke to the scent of guava and the sound of the tide lispingly slurping pebbles. The salt air pried open my lungs. The morning sea was blue: indigo blue, teal blue, metallic blue. I had really made it: I was in Hawaii. And the world was hopeful again, supportive.

I rode my skateboard down the rutted road to Lahaina, a tourist town where vacationers drank gaudy fruit drinks on their hotel verandas. I ate a four-dollar bran muffin and sat under a banyan and thought about what I should do.

There is surf in Lahaina, but the day I arrived, the horizon was dead flat. I checked the newspaper and all the rooms for rent were unaffordable, the hotels more so. I knew from watching surf films that I had to make it to the north shore, the surfer's mecca during the winter swells. But how? Bike? With all my stuff?

The world began to seem cruel and hopeless again.

"Help," I cried to an unknown god, confused and desperate. "Please."

8. I MUST HAVE LOOKED DESPERATE too because, wandering through town past all the damn happy kids with their nice rich (not-divorced) parents, a friendly stranger approached me:

"You lost?"

"You could say that."

"What are you looking for?"

"Well, a lot of stuff. But cheap rent and good surf to start."

"Oh, Paia, man. You gotta go to Paia."

"Are you going?" I asked, thinking at him as loudly as I could: *Please, please offer me a ride.*

"Nah. Too many hippies out there. I'm on vacation with the wife and kids. But it's just on the other side of the island."

9. *Just on the other side of the island.* If he only knew. But I took his advice as an answer to my prayers. And so began my consecutive forty-mile roundtrip bike-rides, ferrying my stuff in batches to the other side of the island. My strategy wasn't elaborate. On each trip, I brought with me a new item. The move took several days and made my knees feel like rusting bolts. But it did force me to let go of some attachments, or, I suppose, exactly one attachment: my skimboard. I gave it to a young Hawaiian boy on a beach near the campground.

"Oh, fo' real, cuz?" the boy said when I handed it to him.

And he ran to show his friends.

10. ON MY FINAL JOURNEY, I pedaled through the Dole pineapple fields: miles of spiky little shrubs that hadn't yet borne fruit. Unfortunately, I had no idea what a ripe pineapple looked like (at the time, I thought they grew under the ground like a potato) so, parched, sun-stroked, sweat-caked, and hauling a backpack full of books and the metal Buddha, I stopped and tried to pick one with my bare hands. Of course, as anyone who has ever tried to uproot a pineapple plant would know, the thing wouldn't budge an inch.

Dirty, angry, and pineapple-less, I groaned the rest of the way through sugar cane fields until I arrived in the land that at this point might as well have been Zion.

Paia was everything I'd imagined. Women with hairy armpits and long skirts roamed mural-lined streets dotted with hemp shops and surf stores. Bearded backpackers played hacky-sack at the bus stop; rusted station wagons bumped over pot-holes; a man with beads in his hair and a nose ring the size of a tennis ball sold beaten travel guides to Bali, Tahiti, Samoa, and Fiji for three bucks each.

"The journey is the destination, man," he said, as I walked by.

"Don't remind me," I said. "You don't know what I went through to get here."

"Right on, man. Keep truckin'."

That day, for $250 per month, I found a plain bed-room in a beach shack where some Australian wind-surfers were living—which is to say passing their days windsurfing, watching cartoons, and drinking a hell of a lot of beer. They were friendly, though. One of them agreed to be my "parent/guardian" so I could sign up at the local high school. "Totally," he said when I suggested the plan to him. I had known him for all of thirty minutes.

The landlord of the beach shack lived there, too. He was a wiry Vietnam veteran who grew pot in the back-yard and looked like an emaciated version of Egon from Ghostbusters. "You sure you're eighteen?" he kept asking, bloodshot eyes squinting behind thick glasses. "I don't want the authorities coming after me."

"I just look young," I assured him.

"Well, I like that you're on a spiritual journey," he said, looking at the Carlos Castaneda book I was reading. "*Don Juan* changed my life."

I smiled. From the looks of him, the book hadn't worked too many miracles. And I didn't tell him that I thought Castaneda was a bit of a crackpot, or that I was on a journey *away from* intoxicants.

But his comment was a nice gesture.

And the place was all I could afford.

11. AFTER I PAID MY RENT and bought some extremely expensive organic groceries—all you could find in town—I had about two hundred dollars left over for survival. So I spent one hundred of them on a 6'6" shortboard. Technically, one should learn to surf on a longboard, but I was far too cool for that. I was an obsessive skater and snowboarder and I figured I would be an absolutely ripping surfer within a few weeks, chumming it up with Kelly Slater and Sunny Garcia by the year's end.

At the surf shop, I tried to play the erudite board connoisseur, employing the lingo I'd learned from *Surfer magazine.* "I want something I can really whip around," I told the shop-owner. "Something with thin rails and a lot of rocker." The owner looked at me (white boy, no tan) suspiciously. "Um, yeah, this is Christian Fletcher's old board," he said, referencing a god-like pro surfer whose poster was pinned up on my bedroom wall back in Sacramento. "It split in the middle, but the repair job is good. Pretty snappy."

For me, this was the surfer equivalent of an aspiring golfer finding Tiger Wood's old clubs at a garage sale.

"Okay," I said, feigning flippancy. "Sure."

12. FROM THAT POINT ON, with the exception of a nice mom donating a whole pizza to me while I was sitting on the beach (I must have looked hungry), I had to pick pineapples (*not* barehanded) and avocados to get any food. I consoled myself by noting the uncanny resemblance between my story and Prince Siddhartha's. My road to sagehood was going according to plan.

Once he left the palace, Siddhartha encountered various meditation teachers and quickly surpassed them in wisdom and skill. Siddhartha saw that these masters were still attaching to certain states of mind and were thus still caught up in the cycle of endless suffering: *samsara*, as it was called in Sanskrit. So he decided to push harder. He hung out with die-hard ascetics for six years, fasting, eating only seeds and roots, and denying himself any healthy sustenance or pleasure. His fasting was so severe that his ribs bulged from his back like a Spanish-tiled rooftop; skin hung off his bones like tinsel. He was near to death—and he realized that even were he to die, it wouldn't much help him end his suffering. (At the time, just about everyone in the area believed in reincarnation so dying would've meant starting over, and maybe as a monkey or a grasshopper.) Eventually, after much time, the prince concluded there was nothing liberating about malnutrition, and he took real food again: a bowl of rice and milk.

13. IMMEDIATELY AFTER PURCHASING the short-board (who knows if it really was Fletcher's?), I walked up the road to a sandy break in town. Coming up the path wearing the closest things I had to surf trunks—I think they were basketball shorts—I could hear it: the repetitive smack and gurgle of big surf. My chest pounded with giddiness.

And then I saw what I had come for: *the North Shore*. It wasn't the north shore of the movies I'd watched dozens of times, the one teeming with pro surfers and full of legendary breaks: Pipeline, Sunset, and Off the Wall. That's on Oahu. But to me, it might as well have been.

The waves crashed and spit and spun. Perfect lines of blue folded over into turquoise walls. Young, tanned surfers skimmed along, spraying peacock tails of water behind them. Some teenage girls in bikinis played smashball on the beach. I tried to flex a little when they looked up at me. They went back to their game.

I jogged into the warm water, unaware that learning on this board on these waves would be like learning to ski on superfast skis on my way down a double black diamond slope. Though if someone had told me, I would've ignored the warning. Tiger sharks could've been circling the break and I would've gone out, dammit. I had waited *eleven freaking years* for this.

LEAVING HOME

As a high school water polo player, I was a fairly strong swimmer. But no amount of pool calisthenics could have prepared me for learning to surf on Maui's north shore in winter. The sea was hungry, and the currents sucked at my ankles.

I lay down on my surfboard and paddled for the horizon, digging my hands in with a big grin. But no sooner had I made a few strokes out then a wall of white foam socked me and sent me flipping backward.

I aimed a smile at the bikini girls.

"Unlucky entry point," I muttered. But when I paddled back out at another point, the same thing happened again—and then again, and then again.

I noticed some of the locals laughing at me—yet another *kook*, as Hawaiians call amateur mainlanders, invading their precious space.

I shrugged off the taunts. I was sure it wouldn't take me long. And I did learn something after a dozen or so times through the washing machine: once hit, struggling only made it worse. Fighting against a wave, I lost all my breath. But if I softened and then surfaced when it let me go, I saved my energy.

14. I WAS FRUSTRATED. I wasn't used to being so *bad* at a sport. I sat on the beach staring at the waves: they had looked so soft and feathery moments ago, now they looked like impenetrable walls, like frothing monsters.

I knew that I needed to learn to *duckdive*, a maneuver in which the surfer presses the entire board a few feet beneath the surface to get under the oncoming surge—but it's not exactly intuitive how to shove a thing buoyant enough to support one's weight under a freight train of rushing water. I pushed down the nose of the board with all my might and the back of the board popped out. Physics. So I tried to jam the back down using my knee or foot, but the nose jutted up. It didn't help that when my eyes met an enormous wave that was about to pound me my brain sent a paralyzing message to my limbs. My eyes squeezed shut and I froze like a cat in a tree.

I spent hours each day at that break, most of it choking on saltwater. Once in a while, there would be a lull and I would make it out with the other surfers—only to realize that I didn't want to be there. I could barely *sit* on the board (the standard position for waiting for waves) and if I couldn't sit on it, there wasn't a chance I was going to *stand* on the thing riding down a vertical liquid wall.

Nonetheless, around the third day, I got it. I really got it. One of the biggest waves I had ever encountered reared in front of me—snarling. I can't tell you how big because even small waves seemed three stories tall during this learning period. (They were probably about three feet.) At any rate, it looked hopeless. The lip plunged toward me, but surprisingly, I didn't freeze. I kept my eyes on the clarity of the water. I pushed the nose of my board under, deep. I crammed the tail of the board down with my knee as if I was trying to force open a locked door. I braced myself. But it was as if the impenetrable wall had melted; my board submerged and I was sucked down, under, and through—effortlessly. I popped up on the other side, turning my head from side to side. Why wasn't I ten feet back in the other direction?

And that's when it all kind of clicked. There was *a way*, a method that worked. The walls were not impenetrable. I realized in that moment that all the initial poundings had scarred me, in a way. I had known intellectually that if I did this duckdiving thing right, it was possible to get through even very big waves. But I'd started believing I couldn't do it. And so I couldn't.

But now I had experienced it.

And I knew.

15. YEARS LATER, an oceanography professor taught me how to better understand what these strange walls of water actually were.

Waves begin with wind blowing on the surface of the water, which creates ripples. Those ripples become like little sails that catch more of the wind's force and transfer it into bigger ripples. The bigger lumps eventually garner speed and spread out, turning into swell.

The swells move through the sea in a complex spiraling motion that gives them "feelers" or "legs." When a swell moves through shallow water (approximately only twice as deep as the swell is tall) those feelers touch the reef, sandbar, or rocks, and the swirling energy "trips." The top of the swell continues at the original velocity while the bottom part stops short, causing the swell to heave up and over itself and pitch into a breaking wave.

The theatrical performance creates the illusion of a fixed entity, a "wave" made of water, which has traveled miles to its destination. But really, the wave is a domino effect of energy, a series of causes and conditions. In essence, the wave is the memory of wind energy transferring between water molecules. Very little water is actually moving. A wave is at once real (real enough to pound rocks to sand) and completely different in every second. Though the wave is definitely real, and appears solid, it is also something of an illusion. (Jumping ahead a little bit, I could also

16. IN MY GRANDIOSE WAY, I figured my duckdiving insight was kind of like Prince Siddhartha's first big step toward enlightenment: a micro-version, but still, a step in the right direction. After hanging with the ascetics, Siddhartha was frustrated: "By this racking practice of austerities I have not attained any superhuman distinction in knowledge and vision worthy of the noble ones. Could there be another path to enlightenment?" Seeking other avenues, he finally discovered the middle way and accepted an offering of food from a village girl. The curmudgeonly ascetics called him a cheater. With newfound strength from nourishment, Siddhartha resolved to end suffering once and for all. He vowed to sit under a bo tree in lotus posture and not get up until he had seen through suffering and its causes. It is said that while he was deep in meditation, Mara, the demon king, tried to distract the prince from his *samadhi*, his meditative focus, creating grand illusions: armies of darkness to scare him and fair maidens to tempt him. But Siddhartha was undeterred. He touched the earth and said, "With the earth as my witness. I am not moved by the demons."

Who knows what Siddhartha saw the night of his enlightenment? But he came out of the whole experience in awe: "Wonder of wonders!" he declared under the bo tree. "Intrinsically all living beings are buddhas, endowed with wisdom and virtue, but because people's minds have become inverted through delusive thinking they fail to perceive this."

He also emphasized that everything is like an illusion, a dream, a mirage. "Suppose, monks," the Buddha later told his students, "that in the last month of the hot season, at high noon, a shimmering mirage appears. A man with good sight would inspect it, ponder it, and carefully investigate it, and it would appear to him to be void, hollow, insubstantial. For what substance could there be in a mirage? So too, monks, whatever kind of perception there is, inferior or superior, far or near: a monk inspects it, ponders it, and carefully investigates it, and it would appear to him to be void, hollow, insubstantial. What substance could there be in perception?"

I often was baffled by the Buddha's statements like this, but out there on the water, I could imagine he could see all the myriad waves of samsara the way I was learning to see the waves of the ocean: penetrable, composite, nonthreatening—in short, saltwater.

17. I WAS HAPPY I was learning to surf. Goal number one was being accomplished. Back on land, though, I had problems. I was running out of money and I was beginning to miss my family and friends. It had been ten days since I'd left home and it felt like three months. One desperate night when the landlord was frightening me with nostalgic stories from 'Nam and the '60s, I called my mom.

And I broke.

I gave up my secret, the last remnant of my power: my location. But not all of it. I told my mom I was living on one of the Hawaiian islands, but I wouldn't tell her which. That way, I figured she wouldn't call in the Navy SEALs after me (when your dad is a colonel, you take precautions).

"Hello."

"Mom. It's me."

"Oh my God, Jaimal! Wait, don't hang up!"

"Mom, calm down. I'm fine. I just wanted to tell you I'm in Hawaii."

"You're not at a friend's house?"

"No. You didn't believe me?"

"Well, the cops thought... Okay, I'm just glad you're okay. I'm just glad—are you okay?"

"I'm fine. Everything's great."

I told her I was staying with a responsible landlord and some nice Australian boys. I told her I had signed up for high school, that I was applying for jobs.

"Really? That's amazing," she said, and her tone relaxed. But then I told her I was learning to surf, and she freaked. "Don't you go out alone!" she said. "Find a buddy!" (To this day, I get the same speech, by the way.)

I usually hated my mom's safety lectures. She was always cutting out news clippings of snowboarders who had died on the trail and giving me the stay-in-bounds speech. It was so annoying. But after a week without a home-cooked meal, I actually missed them… a little.

"No, Mom, I found a couple guys to surf with," I lied. "I'm *fine*. I'll call you back in a few days."

"Jaimal, wait!"

"Mom, I gotta go. I'll call you soon."

I hung up. But I had a queasy, knotted up feeling in my chest. I was so alone. Even the warm Hawaiian air felt cold.

I wanted to be like Siddhartha, unmoved by all the demons. But I didn't even know what my demons were anymore. Just a phone call to my mom made me want to cry. It was slowly dawning on me that, no matter how much I wanted running away to be an act of buddhahood, it was very far from being anything of the sort.

I needed help, guidance, refuge.

18. MY PARENTS BOTH MEDITATED when I was growing up. As a young boy, I occasionally tried it with them. Very quickly, I decided it was *incredibly* boring. Whenever Ciel and I tried it with them at the same time, we'd eventually open our eyes and start giggling uncontrollably. Then we'd get kicked out of the meditation room.

I didn't want to meditate.

But one day, when I was about nine, my dad came back from a work trip to Japan with a statue of Amida Butsu, Amitabha Buddha, the Buddha of the Pure Land, of compassion. He was a perfectly symmetrical shiny black Buddha with an expression of pure serenity. My dad didn't bring the Buddha back for me, but I adopted him anyhow. There was something about the statue that made me want to bring it with me everywhere. At one point, I ran up to my room with the statue and closed the door and tried to mimic the Buddha's posture and expression. I figured his mind was somewhere very nice and I tried to picture that place: waterfalls, green grass, white birds. I tried to soar over the place like a bird. After about three minutes, my dad burst into my room, "Hey, are you meditating in here?"

He wasn't upset. But I was embarrassed that I'd stolen away with the Buddha. I put the statue behind me and looked at him with guilty eyes: "No," I said. "Just sitting here."

After that, I stopped trying to mimic the Buddha. As I got older, I decided religions in general were pretty dumb and dogmatic and that I didn't need any of them. The Buddha's story still intrigued me, but the actual meditation practice seemed a waste of time and reminded me too much of my parents.

Now, though, after the phone call to my mom, I realized I needed *something*.

So I decided to give meditating a try again. I found a secluded spot under a tree and went through the same routine the Buddha had. I vowed to myself, *"I will not move from this spot until I have ended suffering."*

I sat very upright and waited. But after about thirty minutes, my left knee felt like it would go up in flames. Continuing to sit seemed like it would only create more suffering, at least for my knee, so I reneged on my vow. And I decided to sit for only twenty minutes at a time.

I began with the technique of sitting still and counting my breath (inhaling, *one*, exhaling, *one*; inhaling, *two*, exhaling, *two*…) that I'd learned in a yoga class. I was confident, just like when I first paddled out. But getting to breath ten was almost impossible for me. For one thing, I could hear the Aussies always blasting the Cartoon Network from the living room. But even when they weren't, I could rarely make it to ten without my mind wandering into chatter:

*Where was that Hawaiian Tropic model I was sup-
posed to meet? What were my friends saying about
me? How long would it take me to be a pro surfer?*

It was probably because I thought of surfing constantly, but I immediately connected meditation with
paddling out. Sitting was at least as hard. My body
resisted stillness and I was bulldozed by thoughts. The
thoughts were like those impenetrable walls of water,
no, like storm waves with no space in between. In my
muddled mind, there were no clean lines to read, no
chance of duckdiving.

All this time I had thought that "I" was doing the
thinking, that I was perfectly in control. But just like
the sea doesn't control the waves, my thoughts
seemed to move on their own. A Zen meditation book
I read in a bookstore instructed, "Simply observe your
thoughts like water in a river, like clouds passing in an
empty sky." That sounded nice—but watching my
scattered thoughts was more like being an amateur
stenographer during a Congressional debate: "Um,
excuse me, people, yeah, could you just slow down a
lit—*Excuse me! Please!*"

But after a few days, I could get to ten. And then
twenty. And then, very occasionally, one hundred.
And the more I focused, the more my breath became
smooth, almost soothing. And the more my breath
smoothed, the more space there was between thought
waves. I realized my thoughts were connected to my

breath like waves are to wind. If my breath was forced, shallow, quick, or panicked, my thoughts were scattered and out of control. But as my breath calmed, it was as if the onshore winds (which make the ocean's surface choppy) began to fade. The waves were still churning, but they were coming in more clearly with enough space between to see them: coming into being, passing away, dissolving into the ocean of mind.

Anicca, the Buddha called this: impermanence.

19. I HADN'T DONE MUCH OF IT. But even in the very first stages of meditation, I could begin to see thoughts for what they were. Just as a wave does not have a static fundamental substance but is energy transferring between molecules, my feelings and thoughts were a chain of reactions, each dependent on the previous one. I could let them flip me around, spin me out into endless reactions, or let them pass over me—dissolve.

This was revolutionary: it gave me choice.

I realized that I had fled home in the grip of several storm waves: anger, shame, fear, and longing to be somewhere (and someone) else. All these negative waves had been breaking on me all at once. I had hardly been able to breathe. Geographical escape had seemed the only option. But maybe if I had been calmer, if I had learned this meditation thing beforehand, I might have seen other options, might have avoided creating so much worry.

Or not. I really don't know.

But either way, suddenly, guilt set in. I pictured my family huddled around a telephone waiting for my call, hoping I hadn't drowned.

And again, I called home.

20. "Mom, I…"

"Oh my god, Jaimal—it's you! I'm glad you called. This is urgent."

"I know, I…"

"Jaimal. Pa is there! He's looking for you! He flew to Oahu when I told him you were in Hawaii."

"Wait. What?"

"Pa's there! He's scouring the beaches looking for you."

"Oh my… Really?"

"Yes really."

"Shit. Really?"

"Yeah. He's worried, Jaimal. We're all worried. We can't sleep."

"Okay, um, can you hold on?" Hand over mouthpiece: "Fuck. Fuck. Fuck!" Hand off mouthpiece: "Okay, uh, do you have his hotel's number?"

I had planned on telling Mom where I was. But I had not planned on meeting with my dad. My dad, who Ciel and I call Pa, is not a nightmare military dad. He's not a drill sergeant. He's not homophobic. He doesn't think war is the answer and he doesn't have a case of guns. Actually, before going into the Air Force, he was a gourmet chef at a health food restaurant. He and my mom lived in an ashram in the '70s. His favorite pastimes are gardening, cooking, reading books on Buddhism, and listening to jazz. He's a bohemian trapped in a colonel's body. But when he wants to—and especially after a few scotches—he can play the stern colonel very well. And he can *lecture*. He can be such a damn know-it-all. And I didn't want to deal with him, not now.

But I couldn't very well let him roam the beaches of Oahu in a frenzied panic, tapping every curly-haired teenager on the shoulder.

I called his hotel.

21. I COULD REMEMBER GREAT TIMES WITH PA. The memories were opaque, distant. But they were there: sepia prints in a disorganized box of dusty photos. In my memories, Pa and I were almost always at the beach. Pa loved the beach, maybe more than I do. If it was warm, we were in the water, laughing. If it was cold, Pa had a big walking stick and he was finding the best shells.

But those days were over. The more recent memories were of Pa missing my soccer games; Pa coming home tired from work and going in his room to watch TV; Pa drinking too much and fighting with Mom about the most arbitrary topics. After the divorce, he remarried and was much happier. But I only saw him two weekends a month. Occasionally, he would suggest that I go into the military and I would cringe. Did this guy even know me at all? Had he failed to notice that I thought war, as an option for any dispute, ever, was wrong? Had he noticed that he himself often hated his job?

"The military's been good to me," he would say. "You meet a lot of good people."

I told him I would think about the Coast Guard.

The older Pa got, the more politically conservative he became. We didn't agree on most things. And so we learned together to never bring up politics. We almost never spent father-son time unless we were stuck in the car, driving.

22. BUT THIS SEARCHING BUSINESS was different. He was trying to reach out. It was just a feeling I had, but I suddenly believed he really wanted to make amends. Maybe I'd even come to Hawaii, subconsciously, to get his attention. He answered the phone in his hotel room when it rang.

"Hello."

"Hi, Pa," I said, trying to sound cheerful, normal.

"Jaimal!" he said in a strangely exuberant tone. "Well, this is a surprise. So how are you?"

"Uh, good. You?"

"Not bad. I take it you're not in Honolulu."

"Um, yeah, uh… no. Not in Honolulu. But, um, let me see, how should I say this? …You want to come to Maui?"

23. BEING A FORMER HAWAII RESIDENT HIMSELF, I think my dad realized the delicacy of the situation: it was a hostage negotiation. I was the hostage. Hawaii was the kidnapper. Flawless diplomacy was called for.

The following day, Pa pulled up to my beach shack grinning out of a Dodge Neon, looking beachy: sun-burned nose, sunglasses, sandals, surf trunks, baseball cap. We embraced. We smiled.

It was good to see him, good to see a familiar face.

"So, yeah… this is where I live," I said, pointing to a house that looked as if it would soon compost into the red dirt.

"Nice place… homey."

"Yeah, I got a surfboard, too. And a bike."

"Oh yeah. Your mom mentioned the surf—"

"Yeah, she's flipping out about it."

"So, you're all moved in, I guess."

"Yup, all moved in."

We stood with our hands in our pockets. Shoulders slumped. No eye contact.

"Do you want to see my room?"

"Nah, that's okay."

"Sure?"

"Yeah." And then silence.

Uncomfortable silence.

More uncomfortable silence.

"I was thinking," Pa finally said. "Why don't you get your surfboard. And we'll drive to this place—

have you heard about it?—Hana. I hear there's some good waves over there."

This was an incredibly skillful move. Suddenly, my dad was on *my* team: a fellow surfer. (Maybe he knew me better than I thought.) And even if he was just trying to bribe me into coming home, I was up for a trip to Hana. The winds had picked up in Paia, and the surf was junk. There was a good chance that Hana, on the other side of mountains, would be sheltered.

I ran in to grab my stuff and told the Aussies (none of whom had cars or incomes) that I was *driving* to Hana.

"Lucky bastard," said one without looking up from the cartoons.

"Oh, fuck off," said the other.

Those guys were beginning to grow on me.

24. MY DAD IS A MAN OF FEW WORDS and often our time together feels like watching a silent film—but one where you haven't been notified the film is silent and so you keep expecting the characters to speak. No matter how many times I'd thought we were on the verge of developing normal social skills, deep father-son heart-to-hearts, we never did. This was going to be the first time, as far as I could recall, that he and I had spent an extended length of time together.

Fortunately, the Hana Highway is extremely narrow and requires every ounce of the driver's concentration. You have to honk as you go around corners just to avoid head-on collisions. And in the tradewinds, the Neon seemed like it would lift off and blow into the surf.

We stared forward in silence, thinking of things we could say and not saying them. Pa clenched his jaw so his temples throbbed. I hated that. He was mad. What could I say?

But eventually Maui filled the silence. We stopped to watch Haipua'ena Falls rush into a pool of emerald water. We listened to our voices echo off the walls of Honomanu Bay. We watched the surf beating against the Ke'anae Peninsula. Relieved to have nature between us, we talked: about the tall bamboo, the wild orchids, the twisting banyans. *Things* were good to focus on.

They made us feel closer.

25. PA ACTUALLY HAS A KNACK for adventures. In the Azores, he seemed always to have been finding secret coves and old ruins. We hadn't been on any adventures like that in a long time. But when we finally got to Hana, he did it again. Wandering down unmarked back roads, we found a bamboo-shrouded cove where the clearest water in the entire ocean seemed to live. Waves broke over an incandescent reef padded with pockets of white sand. Without a guide-book, we had somehow stumbled onto the perfect surf break.

"Looks like we found your spot," my dad said, grinning. He seemed happier to be in Hawaii than I was.

A few surfers bobbed in the water, riding waist-high waves. After Paia, paddling out in Hana felt like catching dragonflies in a cool meadow. In fact, you could walk to the break. I even stood up *on my surf-board, on the wave!* A Hawaiian woman who resembled the actress who played Keani in the '80s film *North Shore* (about whom I'd been fantasizing intensively over the past two weeks) paddled up to me and told me I was doing "pretty good for a beginner." I could have died happy.

After a while, my dad swam out and fooled around on my board. Not having surfed in some twenty-five years, and having been raised in the longboard era, he looked for all the world like a deranged penguin.

"No wonder you're having so much trouble," he said. "You're trying to float on a potato chip."

We laughed. "And you look like you forgot how to swim," I chuckled. "You're gonna sink that thing."

We traded the board back and forth for about half an hour, both of us doing a pathetic job. And then, out of nowhere, I noticed something weird: *we were having fun*—the two of us, my dad and I, together.

If I stopped to think about it, I'd have to admit that I was still angry with my dad for not coming to many of my soccer or baseball games when I was little. But I guess this wasn't exactly his fault. He just didn't play or have much interest in these sports. Instead, he taught me about cooking and told me Eastern philosophy stories. But at seven, I wanted to play soccer, not learn to make wasabi mashed potatoes and talk about Lao Tzu.

But as I watched him paddling around on my board now, I realized Pa might be trying to make up for those missed games, maybe for all the bad times.

A bumbling turtle floated by, nibbling on seaweed. Parrotfish and clownfish darted behind shoaling coral.

I looked around at Hawaii, at the Pacific, and felt a lump in my throat.

"Thank you," I whispered.

26. Of course, we eventually had to talk about what the hell I was going to do with myself. I was in the middle of a probation sentence for that DUI and I knew my dad was freaking out inside about me developing even more of a criminal record. I was trying not to think about it. But I was pretty scared, too.

"These computers don't forget you," my dad had said when I started my six months of monthly visits to a probation officer. "They *do not* forget!"

But I didn't want to give in and leave Hawaii. I didn't want to be weak.

On our drive back, Pa initiated the peace talks. "I know you want to stay here," he said, "and I understand why. Hell, I want to stay here. But if you're going to leave home, you have to do it in an honest way. This probation thing could really screw you over for a long time."

I stared out the window. I didn't know what to say.

But then he told me he hadn't yet called my probation officer (who wasn't the most caring of women) and that there was still time to get back for my appointment as if nothing had happened.

Damn he was good. First the surf trip to Hana, and now he was putting himself firmly on the rebel team. I flashed to Patrick Swayze in *Point Break*: "This is about us against the system." My dad was not stupid.

I knew he was right. And I think at that moment I decided to come home. But I didn't want to make it that easy for him. I stayed silent. I was still bitter.

"You know, I ran away from home when I was about your age." (Oh great, I thought, here comes the sitcom lecture. Fade in Hawaiian slack-key guitar.) "I was like Huck Finn. I ran away on a river boat and got a job washing dishes."

"Really?" I was genuinely shocked.

"I wanted my independence. I'd been working since the age of thirteen. But I wanted something else, I don't know, a real adventure."

"Well, did you go back?"

"I think I lasted about as long as you have. A couple of weeks. But I realized I should finish high school." He paused. "Look Jaimal, I'm not mad at you. And I don't blame you. But we've got to do this the right way. Why don't you come back and stay with me for a semester. Get away from your friends and your school. For your senior year, we can arrange for you to do something you want—when you're not on probation. Maybe you can come back to Hawaii. We can look into boarding schools."

I closed my eyes. I was still angry at him. He'd screwed up too many times. I wanted to scream, "Fuck you. What do you know about me? And what do you know about commitment? You couldn't even make your marriage work!"

27. THAT NIGHT, WE WENT TO DINNER at a fancy restaurant called Mama's Fish House, the place I had been planning to work at as a bus boy. It was still a little awkward between us. But other than the ocean, one of the few things my dad and I bond around is good food. So for a couple hours, the silence was filled with seafood, then dessert, coffee. The more we ate, the more we relaxed. We told stories about the Azores: about that noisy shoe store, about our Dutch friend Core who built the largest trimaran in the world and circumnavigated the globe, about the time a rogue wave nearly carried me out to sea but my dad caught me and wouldn't let go of my hand. We ate and ate. And Pa ordered a shot of Anisette, the licorice-flavored liqueur he used to drink in the Azores. He said he hadn't had any since.

After dinner we walked along the beach under the bright moonlight and smoked cigars and didn't say much. Just took in the island night.

Normally my dad wouldn't have let me smoke a cigar. In fact, I had never even seen him smoke one either. But it was a special occasion. And neither of us would say it straight, but we both knew the occasion wasn't that I was coming home. The occasion was we were getting to return, albeit briefly, to that space in our hearts when we lived on an island in the middle of the sea, around the corner from the beach, and the family was whole.

Part II
ZEN AND SURFING: A BRIEF HISTORY

'A 'one hua o ka mai'a i ka la ho'okahi 'A 'ohe pala naio.
All knowledge is not taught in the same school.
—Hawaiian proverb

Studying about Zen should never be confused with practicing Zen, just as studying aesthetics should not be confused with being an artist.
—T.P. Sakulis

1. AFTER SIDDHARTHA'S ENLIGHTENMENT, he wasn't sure if he should try to teach what he'd found out under the bo tree. It just seemed somehow ineffable. And if he did teach, who would understand? So he decided against trying to tell anyone what he'd realized. But then the god Brahma Sahampati came down from the heavens and implored the Buddha, saying that his teachings would be a great boon for living beings everywhere throughout all times and places. "Open the door to the deathless!" Brahma had exhorted. "Let them hear the Dharma that the Stainless One has found." In short, as the ancient texts tell us, Brahma talked the Buddha into teaching, and so began a forty-year series of lectures that the Buddha delivered around India to people of all castes and faiths.

The Buddhist sutras are longer than the entire works of Shakespeare and the Bible combined, but one of the teachings that is central to the Zen school is actually one of the very simplest: a group of monks and nuns and laypeople had gathered to hear the Buddha again speak eloquently of the Dharma, but the Buddha said nothing and just held up a flower.

The monks were confused. Was the Buddha stalling? Was this a joke? But one monk, a very wise disciple named Kashyapa, smiled, at which point the Buddha finally spoke, declaring that Kashyapa had understood the day's teaching. He said Kashyapa should forever be known as Mahakashyapa, or "Great Light." And many say that Mahakashyapa understood the highest wisdom of the Buddha in that moment: that the "true mind," the mind that is free of selfishness, cannot be described with words. Or, as some would put it, Kashyapa received the direct mind-to-mind transmission from the Buddha, becoming the first ancestor in what would come to be the Zen lineage.

In the centuries after the Buddha's death, his followers created rifts and various Buddhist schools—Theravada and Mahayana being just two of the biggest divisions—each claiming to be the authentic one. As I mentioned earlier, the Zen tradition (or Chan as it is known in China) officially formed when one school traveled, via the South Indian monk named Bodhidharma, to China around the fourth or fifth century CE. In China, the elaborate Indian Buddhist philosophical systems merged with the simple, grounded Confucian and Taoist philosophies, and flourished, developing into the dynamic Zen tradition whose aesthetic and literature has become so popular in the West. Zen is perhaps most famous for its vexing system of teaching stories and seemingly unanswerable questions, called koans. Many people have heard of the koans "What is your Original Face, the one you had before your parents were born?" and "What is the sound of the Single Hand?" But the following koan neatly summarizes something important about Zen:

One day, two meditation students were looking at a blowing flag and debating a philosophical point. One said the flag was moving. The other said the wind was moving. At that point their teacher, the Sixth Ancestor of Zen, Hui-neng, an illiterate wood-cutter who had been enlightened upon hearing a single line from the Diamond Sutra, said they were both wrong: "The mind is moving," he said.

This is the essence of Zen. ("Mind precedes all things," the Buddha said.) And though trying to intellectually grasp what Hui-neng meant in the deepest sense, at least by the likes of me, may cheapen the insight, I can only guess he was getting at the same point the modern Zen teacher Hakuun Yasutani was in using his wave metaphor: much like a wave is part of, and dependent on, the sea, our individual minds are part of, and dependent on, a larger mind, or substratum that constitutes what we call reality. And though we perceive our minds as separate from others and from the rest of reality, it is actually the case that just as a wave cannot exist apart from water, what we mistake as "our" minds are dependent on the one true mind, the Buddha mind. In one sense, as I understand it, the "objective" of Zen meditation is not to nullify or stop the functioning of our small mind in favor of some imagined "other" mind, the Buddha mind, but to recognize that the source of our mind is itself the Buddha mind, and our individualistic thinking is the very functioning of the Buddha mind. ("Waves are the practice of water," said Suzuki Roshi. "To speak of waves apart from water or water apart from waves is a delusion.")

Zen teachers all seem to say similar things about our true mind: they say it is fundamentally whole, that it is empty of inherent characteristics and yet is not nothingness. It is formless, yet takes form in everything. It is "vast and spacious," wrote master Hung-chih, "like the sky and water merging during autumn." And Chuang-Tzu, who was not a Buddhist but a Taoist who greatly influenced Zen, once said: "Pour into it and it is never full, dip from it and it never runs dry."

In that way, I suppose, it's like the sea.

2. ODDLY ENOUGH, surfing may be about the same age as Zen. Just about the time Bodhidharma showed up in southern China, the Polynesians, largely regarded as the most deft sailors ever, were navigating by the stars to Hawaii, where surfing was most likely born. It's hard to say when the first surfer rode a wave in Hawaii, as the Hawaiians had no written language until the nineteenth century. But the West discovered the sport in 1778 when the British seaman Captain James Cook made the first recorded journey to the Hawaiian islands. After observing a native riding a canoe in the surf, Cook wrote: "I could not help concluding that this man felt the most supreme pleasure while he was driven on so fast and so smoothly by the sea."

For the Hawaiians, it seems surfing was a sport, a spiritual rite, and a form of play, all at once. The system of taboos (in Hawaiian, *kapu*) regulated who could surf, how to surf, where to surf, how to read weather patterns, how to make surfboards, and how to convince the gods to make the surf good. Women, children, and commoners surfed for fun. But riding big waves was also a way the *ali'i*, the chiefs, demonstrated their clout. When the surf was too big even for the chiefs, it was called *'Awili*, a word which meant that the gods were surfing.

In the 1800s, Calvinist missionaries to Hawaii outlawed surfing because it seemed to them like frivolous wantonness. While they were at it they also out-lawed the wearing of only loincloths and female-male mingling. (I imagine these guys would be disturbed to learn that there are now quite a few Christian surfing organizations.) One missionary of that period preached that "the decline and discontin-uation of the use of the surfboard, as civilization advances, may be accounted for by the increase in modesty, industry, and religion."

Western colonization was hard on Hawaii. Surfing became nearly extinct. The native Hawaiian popula-tion perished in droves, falling to Westerner-imported syphilis, gonorrhea, and leprosy. Hawaiians gradually lost much of their land and all their autonomy when the U.S. annexed Hawaii as a territory in 1898 (later, in 1959, Hawaii became the fiftieth state). Many of the native Hawaiian customs have since died out or survive in performance-forms only, as eye-candy for tourists.

But surfing did end up surviving, though perhaps narrowly. Much as the Zen tradition has remained resilient through horrible political unrest and anti-religion regimes in China, surfing not only survived in Hawaii, it spread across the entire globe. In the early years of the twentieth century, surfing got break-out attention through Olympic swimmer and native Hawaiian Duke Kahanamoku's international surf demonstrations.

3. THINGS HAVE CHANGED A LOT since the first bald-headed monks wandered China in their tattered robes, or the first Polynesians carried their thick balsawood boards down to the shoreline. And with a competitive multi-million-dollar surf industry and a Zen tradition more familiar as advertising hook than an actual practice, one could argue that both have lost their souls.

One could argue that—but in my opinion, one would be wrong.

It seems to me that as long as there are humans, we will search for freedom in every means available to us. I've looked around a fair bit; and Zen and surfing still seem pretty damn good.

Part III
MONKHOOD

For a deed to be totally pure, it must be done without any thought of reward, whether worldly or divine. It is this kind of deed which is called a "deed of merit." And because no merit is sought, it is a deed of immeasurable merit, of infinite merit.
—Thich Thien-An

1. YUBA CITY IS A SMALL TOWN with big soybean fields and an Air Force base called Beale. It neighbors Marysville, one of the crystal-meth capitals of the country. Pa and Linda, my stepmom, lived in a brand-new Yuba City tract home next to a sewage plant. It was a pretty home, and Pa did his best to make it comfortable for us, planting a huge flower garden and installing a gazebo with a hot-tub. But during those scorching valley days, the whole neighborhood smelled like sewage, a scent that no amount of flowers could hide.

It wasn't so bad—though neither was it what I'd had in mind when I traded in my Hawaiian-surf fantasy for a law-abiding probationer's life. Fortunately, Yuba City had a new skateboard park with lots of concrete wave-like structures. I spent hours thrashing around the park on my old skateboard, pretending the concrete was saltwater and the soybeans were pineapples. I got by.

And it was temporary—*thank God* it was temporary. My parents held up their end of the bargain, though since boarding school in Hawaii was too expensive, they let me choose any other destination for my senior year. I ended up planning a year in France through a discount student exchange program.

Where in France I would end up depended on where the program could find me a host family. I prayed and prayed to be placed in Biarritz, the Huntington Beach of France, and imagined myself shredding waves off topless beaches or sipping a morning espresso with my feet in the sand. I got *le Banlieue*.

The word means "suburb" but in Paris it has come to be synonymous with "ghetto"—and I quickly saw why. I had a host-family brother who loved stealing cars and collecting weapons, and a host-mother who made me pay her five francs if I ever had my hands in my pockets around her (because somehow it meant I wasn't ready to work at the snap of her finger). One time, I actually got mugged for, of all things, a fruit-cake. But the final straw came when I learned my host-mother was stealing minutes from my phone card.

I managed to get a new host-family, and swapped the ghetto for a bucolic town on the Swiss-French border. No beaches for hundreds of miles, but at least I could try to live out some of my surfing fantasies on a snowboard in the Alps. In Lons le Saunier, I continued my daily twenty-minute zazen periods, often riding my bike into the rolling wood to sit.

But my formal introduction to Zen didn't begin until I visited a Zen monastery in the southwest town of Bordeaux, a place called Le Village des Pruniers, or Plum Village.

2. AN OLD VIETNAMESE MASTER named Thich Nhat Hanh lived at the village. I'm sure you've heard of him. Besides the Dalai Lama, Thich Nhat Hanh is the most well-known Buddhist teacher in the West. He's perhaps most famous for his efforts to ground Buddhism's high-minded compassion in everyday situations and societal concerns.

Thay, as his students call him, was a monk in Vietnam during the America-Vietnam war. Watching his beloved country go up in napalm flames, he and his fellow monks decided to break with their ritual hours of still meditation to help the war victims all around them. They rebuilt destroyed villages and nursed the injured and dying. For the crime of publicly opposing the war, Thay was exiled from his native land. He went to France.

I'd read just about all Thay's books: *Being Peace* and *The Miracle of Mindfulness* particularly had changed my life profoundly. When I finally saw him speak, I was expecting to see a halo around his head, or lightning from his fingertips, or something somehow suitably grand. Mainly, though he was just much smaller than I'd expected: seventy-three years old, frail, bald, and I think not much more than one hundred pounds. His skin seemed to have a softness about it, and so did his eyes. He looked almost like a child. But there was something about him, something very soft and placid.

Thay spoke on compassion the day I came. I don't remember the talk, but I do vividly remember a question he took after it. The questioner, who identified himself as an American Vietnam War vet and looked about my father's age, said that he had accidentally killed Vietnamese children during the war and could not forgive himself. He could barely sleep. He wanted to make peace with the Vietnamese and with himself—"But how?" he asked.

Thay sat cross-legged in a dark brown robe, the color of the Bordeaux dirt, rich and almost black. He smiled, pondered briefly, then said slowly, as is his custom, "You cannot change the past. But there are Vietnamese children alive today who are sick, who are dying. I think you can help save those children who are still alive. Do this, and you honor the lives of all children who have been killed."

The man bowed his head deeply. I think he cried.

Then Thay said one other thing that still comes back to me often: Speaking of the different types of compassion, he said, "We can help others like the right hand helps the left hand." He chuckled at his little metaphor. "The right hand does not think, 'I should help the left hand, that is the right thing to do.' It simply acts. Because it knows the two hands depend on each other."

Hearing Thay say this, it was as if everything I'd been reading finally made sense. He summarized it all in a few simple words. But it wasn't even what he said. It was how he said it, how he moved. What his being exuded. I had never seen such peace and kindness on a human's face. I decided that day that I would be a Buddhist monk, too.

Nothing else mattered but finding for myself the peace Thay so clearly possessed.

3. THAT DAY, I CALLED MY MOM from Plum Village's pay phone. By this point, she'd gotten used to my spontaneous antics and wasn't particularly shocked when I reported a sudden change of plans.

"Hi Mom. Guess what?"

"What?"

"I'm going to be a monk."

"Okay. What made you want to do that?"

"Well, I—a lot of things. But I'm in Plum Village, you know, Thich Nhat Hanh's monastery. And I've decided I don't think I need to finish high school. I mean—"

"Jaimal, you have two months left."

"I know but… It's so amazing here and…"

"Jaimal."

"Okay, okay—but afterward."

"We'll talk about this when you get home."

4. I DID FOLLOW THROUGH on my monastery plan, just not at Le Village des Pruniers. After graduation, I went on a little Buddhist monastery tour of California (there are quite a few) and eventually moved into an orthodox Chinese Buddhist monastery in Berkeley, rooming with another American teenager named Aran.

Aran and I were both enamored with the idea of being Buddhist monks—if not, perhaps, all the rigors of the lifestyle. We wanted to save the world with sublime wisdom, bald heads, and incense offerings. It didn't matter that neither of us had ever been able to stick with anything for longer than a year. *This* was different. *This* was our destiny. We were *certain.*

And we were actually really good pretend monks for a while. For almost a year, we woke every morning at 3:30 for meditation and chanting. We ate one meal a day. We recited sutras. We sat weeks-long meditation retreats where the schedule required fourteen hours per day of sitting. We did tai chi and kung fu and tried to learn Mandarin. We never drank alcohol and rarely spoke to women. We knelt every day and took the impossible vows of the bodhisattva:

MONKHOOD

Living beings are numberless,
 I vow to save them all.
Confusions are inexhaustible,
 I vow to cut them all off.
Dharma gates are boundless,
 I vow to enter them.
The Buddha-way is unattainable,
 I vow to attain it.

5. AT NIGHT, after the evening ceremony, we fantasized about wandering the misty mountains of China with our shaved heads and begging bowls.

"I think we could just live on offerings out there."

"Yeah, climb the five sacred mountains."

"Beautiful in spring."

"Visit Master Hai Deng at Shaolin Temple."

"Learn one-finger handstands."

"Live in caves."

"Write poems with wandering Taoists."

"Play with orphans."

"Eat mooncakes."

6. HENG SURE, THE AMERICAN ABBOT of the monastery, smiled indulgently at our fantasies from time to time. But having been a monk for thirty years, he also knew what it takes to stick with it for real. And he knew us. He eventually offered some advice: "You guys might want to try college first. You know, a lot can change."

So just as we were fully convinced of our utmost monastic purity, just as our moms were beginning to give up on grandchildren altogether, Aran and I went back to the real world, back to the world of paying rent—well, I guess it would be my *first* time paying rent—back to worrying about designer clothing and girls and which music was hip and which new comedian was funniest and which politician the biggest fraud, back to the incessant pounding waves of modern life.

7. IT WAS AWFUL.

MONKHOOD

8. I UNDERSTOOD I WASN'T READY for monkhood, but outside of the safe monastery walls, I felt like flotsam adrift on a stormy sea.

I thought about classes at the community college, but they just seemed trivial compared with misty-mountain searches for enlightenment.

I tried to be normal. But normal was *difficult.*

I got a girlfriend (she broke my heart). I went to parties (they made me tired). I tried to do volunteer work (I got sick).

And that's when they started happening again: the water dreams. They came almost every night, but this time without stories: just crashing waves, floods, tsunamis. And sometimes the water was gentle and warm and peaceful and I woke up feeling better. I gradually was reminded of a vision I'd had of another type of life. It wasn't being a monk, but it also wasn't constrained by the shackles of the modern rat-race: it was the life of a surfer.

And so just months after leaving the monastery, I found myself high above the Pacific, watching those same waterfalls and hula girls on the in-flight television, preparing for yet another trip to Hawaii.

Part IV
POHOIKI

Ike aku, ike mai; kokua aku, kokua mai.
Recognize others, be recognized; help others, be helped.
—Hawaiian proverb

The Supreme good is like water,
which nourishes all things without trying to.
—Lao-Tzu

1. CIEL HAD JUST GRADUATED from college with a degree in English, and leaving the university was for her something like leaving the monastery was for me. She was a lost poet. In her panic, she and a mutual friend of ours found something called an "eco resort" on the rugged southern shore of Hawaii, the youngest and largest island in the seven-island chain. It was called Kalani Honua, Heaven on Earth.

"You can work there twenty-four hours per week," Ciel told me, "and they'll give us room and board."

"Is there surf?"

"Dude, it's Hawaii, freak. Remember—the place you ran away to?"

"Well, I don't want to go to some volcano resort."

"There's a hot-tub. And it's *on the water.*"

And that was all she had to say.

2. "RESORT" WAS NOT QUITE THE RIGHT WORD for Kalani. Jungle commune would have been better. Ciel and I became two of the twenty or so "Work Scholars" who came from around the world with a dream of paradise. And we got a version of it.

We all lived in screened-in A-frame huts in the middle of a rain forest, each hut big enough for a single lamp and a bed. We were told to watch out for scorpions and centipedes in our beds. During the first week, I dreamt I was grabbing onto a pine branch and woke gripping a six-inch centipede. Then it stung me.

As it turned out, heaven on Earth was rustic and it had many more bugs than one might imagine. But for Ciel and me, happy with anything that didn't resemble so-called reality, it was perfect: free yoga classes every morning; three all-you-can-eat vegetarian feasts per day; a pool; and a bunch of lost souls like us trying to forget that they were lost.

At night, our little A-frames glowed like mystical pyramids. Tucked inside, the surf lulled us to sleep and drowned out the chirping tree frogs. On full-moon nights, we all marched down to the cliff above the sea and built a bonfire and told each other Hawaiian myths we'd picked up in tourist books. We hiked to waterfalls, bathed in natural steam vents, swam in warm pools heated by the lava.

And there *was* surf. The break, called Pohoiki, was a long six miles away. I had to strap my board (the same old thruster I'd bought on Maui for a hundred dollars) to a dilapidated beach cruiser with a makeshift duct tape surfboard rack. But the road to the break ran along blackened, volcanic bluffs and there were plenty of lookout points to stop and eat a passion fruit or a mango, which grew wild all along.

3. POHOIKI IS ONE of the most consistent surf spots on the Big Island. It's a series of southeast-facing coves and reefs all angled slightly differently so they can filter both direct south and wrapping northern swells into waves.

It had been about two years since I'd surfed, and the little bit I'd picked up was completely gone. But this time, a little older and wiser (I was, after all, nineteen), I decided to observe for a day before paddling out.

There was a fierce hurricane swell filling the bays when I arrived to watch. There must have been a hundred surfers in the water, eyes all locked on the horizon like members of some odd religious cult awaiting a messiah from the southeast.

I sat on the grass and watched for surfers whose style I planned on emulating. Where did they sit? What kind of boards did they ride? How did they shift their weight on turns? There were so many skilled surfers: burly Hawaiian men with arms bigger than my thighs, tanned teenage girls with tattoos on their ankles, screaming kids on bodyboards, old men with beer-guts, blonde Californian "transplants."

I watched for hours and eventually became entranced with a young Hawaiian surfer on a bright yellow "fish"—a short, stubby board with a split tail. The boy couldn't have been older than fourteen, but he could surf as well as or better than anyone else at

Pohoiki. He was skinny with big black eyes, dark skin, and straight black hair. He wasn't the most acrobatic surfer, but he had a certain ease, a carefree grace, like a tango dancer, and a body that seemed almost Gumby-like.

And it wasn't just his surfing that caught my attention. He was always in the right place at the right time. Before a swell could even be seen on the horizon, the boy would casually paddle to the place the next wave would hit.

Either he was very lucky, or every cell in his body was tuned to the sea.

4. I LATER LEARNED that the boy's name was Kekoa, which means "the brave one." And his skills could be explained by the fact that he had grown up practically in Pohoiki's water. His family owned the only house that sat right on the bay. It was a little red shack that reminded me of a miniature barn, standing humbly in the shade of several palms. Kekoa often woke at sunrise and surfed before school. Then he came home and surfed until sunset, riding a wave in under the last rays of light, just in time for dinner.

I got up the courage to paddle out at Pohoiki the next day; and I kept watching Kekoa. I noticed that a lot of surfers had a hungry glare as they were waiting for waves, as if they needed to get their quota, assert their status in the pack. But Kekoa was always laughing and splashing, teasing his friends with goofy taunts: "Hey brah, dis wave don't like you, bettah take next one."

Then he'd take off on that wave, grinning as he dropped.

5. GENERALLY SPEAKING, there is a deep animosity at surf breaks between locals and newcomers. Locals often get annoyed when out-of-towners crowd their waves, especially out-of-towners who can't surf. Fights often ensue. In Hawaii the animosity is often especially strong between native Hawaiian locals and the *haoles*, the white folks.

I was the lowest of the low: a white boy who couldn't surf. For the first couple weeks at Pohoiki, I felt like I did little but get in the way of better surfers. So I tried to stay clear of the pack, and follow that Hawaiian proverb: "Observe with the eyes; listen with the ears; shut the mouth." But Kekoa, breaking the code of glowering at newcomers, was immediately friendly, always offering a smile, a nod, sometimes even conversation.

"So brah, wha you from?" Kekoa asked me after I'd been surfing Pohoiki for a week. And he must have seen me belly flop on about fifty waves.

"California," I said, embarrassed to be from a place where it is assumed everyone surfs.

"So what? Not much surf where you live?" he teased.

"No, my folks live a little ways from the coast—unfortunately. Snowboarding though. I snowboard a lot. And skate. I'm trying to transfer the skills. Obviously, it's not going so well."

Kekoa's face lit up.

"No way, brah—snow! Ho! I nevah seen snow. Must be so mean. Riding da frozen wave. I watch these guys on TV. So mean."

A couple times, Kekoa even backed off waves and ushered me forward. "Cuz, dis one fo' you. No faceplants. Try focus."

Then I'd faceplant.

6. WHEN I FIRST ARRIVED on the Big Island, a Hawaiian storyteller told me that Pele, the lava goddess, tests visitors to see if they're worthy of her island. Overeager tourists are always getting horribly injured on the lava. And if they have to fly home with a broken arm or a slashed knee, Hawaiians often say Pele sent them back.

I'd thought it was just a legend.

7. ONE DAY, after I'd just started feeling a little comfortable at Pohoiki, I was paddling out over the shallow reef when a crystal-clear wave came toward me. It wasn't big or scary and as it rolled over the shallow reef, the pinks, whites, and yellows of the coral refracted through it: a moving prism. The wave was so beautiful, I think I briefly forgot what I was doing. I duckdove too late and in the wrong spot, so the nose of my board met the reef. My board stopped, but my body kept going. My face was hovering—unprotected—directly over the coral just as the lip of that moving prism broke on the back of my head. My face met the reef like a clove of garlic meeting a garlic press.

Blood clouded the water. Two subsequent waves washed me further onto reef, slicing knees, elbows, toes, with deep razor-thin gashes. I had an image of being spun in a washing machine filled with broken glass.

Gripping my board tightly (it was, after all, the only valuable possession I had in Hawaii), I was finally able to roll off the reef into deeper water and paddle in. My lips were swelling. There was blood dripping from dozens of little scratches. The cuts actually weren't that serious. But I felt stupid. I hadn't even been *riding* a wave. This was not a good way to get in with the locals, I thought to myself as I walked back to my bike. Pele didn't want me. Coming to Hawaii was a dumb idea.

Then I heard the voice of a young kid. "Eh, California." It was Kekoa.

"Reef don't feel like snow, eh brah?"

I couldn't help laughing. Smiling made the cut on my lip open more. I flinched.

Kekoa was holding what looked like a pine cone dipped in gelatin. He tossed it to me and I caught it. It felt like I imagined a recently-living brain would, and smelled like rotting eggs and mucus.

"What is it?"

"*Noni*, brah. Local medicine. Try put on yo' face. Mash it up. Rub it like lotion."

"Thanks," I said, genuinely grateful but a bit apprehensive about rubbing the foul fruit on my skin. "Are you sure, man? You put this on your—" But when I looked up Kekoa was already diving onto his board and paddling back out. He splashed his friend as he paddled by, who was probably making fun of him for helping the clumsy *haole*.

I couldn't help remembering Thich Nhat Hanh's lecture: "The right hand doesn't think, 'I should help the left hand.' It just acts. Because it knows both hands depend on each other."

Part V
WIZARDS AND
WATER-WALKING

*How wonderful are islands! Islands in space, like this one
I have come to, ringed about by miles of water, linked by
no bridges, no cables, no telephones. An island from the
world and the world's life.*
—Anne Morrow Lindbergh

*If I were called in
To construct a religion
I should make use of water.*
—Philip Larkin

1. WATER IS FULL OF MAGIC. Shapeless but incompressible, it is the only substance that can exist naturally as solid, liquid, and gas inside earth's temperature range. It's called the "universal solvent" because it dissolves more substances than any other liquid—and yet is also harmless to drink and ultimately sustains all life. "If there is magic on this planet," wrote naturalist Loren Eiseley, "it is contained in water."

And the sea is rife with magical creatures. As a boy, I studied them in picture books, and often thought I could make out their shadows in the deep: ferocious rhino-like turtles the size of small islands; giant squid thrusting their redwood-sized tentacles through pirate ships; mermaids singing alluring melodies in foreign tongues.

Most of my childhood memories have dissolved, but I do remember vividly the magic of the Azores. Perhaps because of being surrounded by water, islands take on some of water's magic. The tangled fig tree in our backyard was to me and my sister a witch's lair and fire swamp. Fairies hovered in our mom's garden like hummingbirds. Ciel and I caught them in nets, put them briefly in jars, investigated their peculiarities, set them free. Once, Mom even designed silken robes with golden twine belts and we all dressed up like angels to invite goodness into our new home. I didn't see any real angels, but Ciel and I agreed that we felt them fluttering through the windows and all about the ceiling.

When we moved into civilization—Sacramento, capital of the fifth largest economy in the world—sea monsters and fairies took a backseat to basketball games, skateboards, girls. My relationship with the sea and its denizens also seemed to change. I dreamed recurrently of falling off a pier into an ink-black sea writhing with sharks, killer whales, and squid.

I awoke each time in a horrible sweat.

2. YEARS PASSED, AND I "MATURED," rarely thinking of magic or sea monsters. But then I began to practice Zen. And perhaps, one might say, I regressed.

How to explain?

Tom Robbins once wrote that "disbelief in magic can force a poor soul into believing in government and business." And a famous Zen saying comes to mind:

> Before you study Zen, mountains are mountains and rivers are rivers; while you are studying Zen, mountains are no longer mountains and rivers are no longer rivers; after Zen, mountains are once again mountains and rivers again rivers.

After that year in the monastery, I suppose I was in that middle stage—rivers, for me, were no longer rivers. Or maybe it was overexposure to the Hawaiian elements, but I felt the structures that hold reality in place were beginning to crumble. Nothing seemed like what it was. I had fallen into that mental reel that fairy tales and fantasy novels arise out of, perhaps even that place shamans and the mentally ill also inhabit.

I often thought of what Heng Sure, the abbot of the monastery, told me: "At some point in your practice, you realize thoughts are *alive*." I wasn't at that point, but I could see a bit of what he meant. And if thoughts were alive—I thought—then what of those sea monsters in the Azores?

What of my fantasies, dreams, and nightmares?

3. WHEN I ARRIVED AT KALANI, I was trying desperately to integrate what I'd learned at the monastery into everyday life, and I felt like I was failing. I was stuck between worlds. I needed a bridge, a translator, a medium.

And just as I felt completely lost, appropriately, I met a wizard.

His name was Romney. And he moved into the jungle commune shortly after Ciel and I had.

Looking like a younger Gandalf, Rom had long straight hair that had been bleached near white by hours in the sun. His blue eyes tucked under bushy blonde eyebrows. He was only twenty-five or so, but he laughed all the time with what seemed to be a much older man's mirth.

I call him a wizard not because he said so or because he had a secret book of spells, but because Rom could do just about anything he put his mind to. He was a part-time gold-miner from Australia, but he also fixed the old surfboards that I thought would never ride again, turned the rusty beach cruisers into smooth gliding machines, wrote songs, ran triathlons, climbed mountains, built recycling systems, and spoke several different languages. And Rom possessed a quality that was surprisingly rare among our crew of escapees: contentment.

WIZARDS AND WATER-WALKING

But more important to me than any of that: Rom was an adept in the particular magical art that obsessed me—the art of walking on water, the art of surfing.

4. ROM GREW UP DOWN UNDER surfing the shark-infested waters and he had accrued what he called in the Australian vernacular "heaps" of knowledge and skill on the subject. He never sat me down and taught me about how to pop at just the right moment, never gave me surf drills, and never had me master the many different types of surfboards—and yet, being around him great teachings naturally arose.

Occasionally Rom and I would pull our beach cruisers to the side of the road, peel a mango, and talk. Sometimes a pod of dolphins or whales would swim by and we'd ride our bikes along the shore, trying to keep up. Other times, Rom just looked out at the water and didn't say anything.

"What are you looking at?" I asked him one day.

"Reading, mate. Reading the signs." Then he laughed a little, not taking himself too seriously.

"What signs?"

"The clouds, the wind, the ships out there."

"Really, the ships?"

Rom pointed to some ships anchored offshore. Their bows were angled toward Pohoiki. "Anchored ships always turn into the wind. The ships' angle means the winds are offshore, which is good news for us."

"So how do you read the clouds?"

"Sometimes it's just a feeling. I think just watching a lot when I was a little one taught me some of the patterns. Look at—that cloud over there. You see how it's hovering over a point of land in an otherwise cloudless sky? That can mean the wind is blowing over the land instead of around the side of it. And that can help you figure out how the winds are going to change. You'll catch on. Just keep your eyes open, mate."

5. AT THE MONASTERY, many of the core lessons were about the Buddha's teaching of interconnectedness, how everything is linked to everything else, down to the smallest insect or blade of grass, and how failure to respect that interconnection leads only to suffering, both for individuals and societies. I came to see that Rom was teaching me the same concepts in a way I could really connect with, a way that pertained directly to my life now.

Rom explained things like how the moon's gravity pulled the entire ocean into a bulge, so that as the earth rotated, the bulge was pulled and pushed, shaping the tides. He taught me how a storm in Japan could create waves on a beach halfway across the ocean, and how those waves are also affected by the shape of the coastline and the topography of the ocean floor. And that the difference between the temperature of the land and that of the sea creates wind, so sunset and sunrise, the times when everything begins to cool down, the sea is often glassy and best for surfing.

Rom taught me about short- and long-period swells, about the bathymetry of the continental shelf, about deep water canyons and sea mounts.

What I liked most about learning the science of surfing was that even the pure facts were poetic. I began to see why the Hawaiians believed the gods were surfers.

The interplay of waves and wind and sun and moon seemed all too magical to be real.

Once we hit the water, though, the talking stopped.

"No one can teach you to surf," Rom often told me.

We might talk about what the waves were doing, but never about surfing technique. Rom just let me figure it out. Yet over time, I gleaned a couple essentials:

1. Understand your environment as much as possible.
2. Fear *nothing*.

Those were main tenets of the Romney School of Surfing.

6. ROM HAD PLENTY OF SURFING SKILL: balance, agility, speed. But I think fearlessness was at least half of his talent. Not that he was a daredevil, stupidly throwing himself into any situation to prove his manhood. There were plenty of days when Rom knew the surf was beyond his limits, and he humbly declined the waves. But once he'd assessed the situation and decided to go for it, he was committed with every ounce of his being.

The take-off is arguably the most scary and difficult part of riding a wave. Too far forward or back can be the difference between a smooth glide down the face or being pitched—what surfers call "going over the falls." It's best to catch a wave just as it's setting up, when there is enough incline to catch it, but before the wave goes concave. In the take-off, and really throughout the entire ride on the wave, the surfer, like the Zen student, must constantly find the middle way.

The more concave the wave, the more difficult the take-off. Skilled surfers, though, can sometimes literally take off as the wave is breaking and air-drop through the C-shaped section. Sometimes they make it. Sometimes they don't. But once the surfer is beyond a certain point, there is no turning back. Hesitation can make things far worse than complete commitment. And to anyone who has looked down the dredging face of a big wave, especially over Hawaii's shallow reefs, that commitment is impressive.

You couldn't surf with Rom and be lazy. Shacks, Bowls, First Bay, Second Bay, Dead Trees—you had to push. You had to commit.

There's an old Zen saying that you should practice Zen like your head is on fire. Instinctively, with full focus and commitment, and no hesitation. Rom surfed like it was the only thing that could quench the flames.

I did my best to keep up.

7. THERE WAS A BAY just south of Second Bay that we had never surfed and I didn't plan on trying. In fact, many of the local surfers didn't go out there. Third Bay was a deep-water break that only worked with a large, long-period swell, the type Rom said had exceptional power. For Third Bay to be surfable, the face of the wave had to be about ten feet high, minimum. But it got much, much bigger. And if the raw power of the wave wasn't staggering enough, Third Bay's borders were made of razor-sharp lava rock. The wave could toss a 200-pound surfer onto that lava like a crumb flicked off a pinky. When Third Bay was really good, a crowd would line up near the jetty and watch the few local legends pull into the tubes— kinetic vortexes so big a F-150 pickup could pass through them.

I wasn't ready for Third Bay and I knew it. Rom knew it, too. But I suppose he couldn't help himself. "I reckon it can't be that bad, mate," Rom said one night over dinner. "I've been watching it, and on a medium-sized day, even if you fall, you just have to paddle like mad to get out of there so you don't get smashed." (Rom didn't always come off as the wisest wizard.)

"I'm not going out there," said a bodyboarder from L.A., Ryan, who was also doing a stint in the A-frames. "I've heard too many gnarly stories of bodies washing up on the rocks."

"Stories, stories," Rom said. "Every spot has stories. I'm telling you, it's not so bad. Next time it works, I'm going. You boys can come along if you like."

I was silent.

8. ROM HAD A KNACK for getting me to do things I would've never done on my own: scaling Mauna Loa, a 14,000-foot volcano, in a single day; night-diving into caves and crevices where creepy bioluminescent things twinkled like underwater fireflies; Dawn Patrol. The latter happened at least once a week, usually at about 4 AM.

"DAWN PATROL!" Rom would shout at the door of my hut. When I stumbled to the door, one eye open, he would be standing there in blue surf trunks, no shirt, a head-lamp strapped to his forehead, grinning and shoving bananas in his mouth. "Rise and shine, mate! Our baby's calling."

We'd bike in the dark to the break, our surfboards throwing us off balance, and then paddle out into the cold water. It was so black we could barely see the waves.

We would float out there as the moon sank behind the palms—alone except maybe for tiger sharks submerged under the silvery waves—until a huge orange sun rose right out of the sea. Dolphins swam by, coming just inches from our boards.

There was really nothing better in the world.

9. IN ZEN PRACTICE, one is often taught not to *try* to do anything, to surrender, to just be with what is happening moment to moment, to let the present wash over you. It's a bit of a Catch-22 because the retreats in which one is meant to intensively practice this nondoing are *very difficult*. It's hard to stay still for hours at a time. Harder still to resist the urge to run out the door.

The language of "doing nondoing" comes largely out of Taoism, an ancient Chinese philosophy that seems to be modeled almost completely off of observations of the natural elements, particularly the movement of water. "Softness triumphs over hardness," wrote Lao-Tzu, the greatest of Taoist sages. "What is more malleable is always superior over that which is immovable. This is the principle of controlling things by going along with them, of mastery through adaptation."

This was the principal teaching of Dawn Patrol.

10. ON THE USUAL CROWDED DAYS at Pohoiki, I was too self-conscious to actualize these principles. I tried too hard, powering through my turns until I fell, or getting overly excited in crucial situations, hardening instead of relaxing and applying my weight. I wanted so badly to perform well that I'd thrash around on the wave instead of intuitively reacting to its movements.

But on Dawn Patrol with only the sun, Rom, and an occasional pod of dolphins around, I could finally let go a little. And it was surprising what relaxing could do. The steep sections that previously seemed impassable were suddenly passed. It happened just by feeling where the wave was going, and keeping my eye on where I wanted to be.

The modern Zen teacher Taisen Deshimaru described mind and body in Zen like this:

> The body moves naturally, automatically, unconsciously, without any personal intervention or awareness. But if we begin to use our faculty of reasoning, our actions become slow and hesitant.

Or, as the sixteenth-century master Takuan Soho advised a young samurai:

Try not to localize the mind anywhere, but let it fill up the whole body, let it flow throughout the totality of your being. When this happens you use the hands where they are needed, you use the legs and eyes where they are needed, and no time or energy will go to waste.

This is what surfing was starting to teach me.

I still botched plenty of good waves. But it felt like a new type of surfing was starting to be accessible.

"Mate, I think you're beginning to get this."

11. So after twenty or so Dawn Patrols, the dates of which were always determined by Rom's wave readings, I began to trust his judgment, and we both began to trust my surfing. When the day came that the treacherous Third Bay was finally breaking in a manner that didn't look like it would crush us into shark treats (with scant waves of, say, only twelve-foot faces), it only took a little arm-twisting from Rom to pique my interest.

"It can't hurt to check it out," Rom said, "Let's just have us a look-see."

Ryan and I agreed to have a look—*only* a look. We paddled through First Bay, stopping at Second Bay to catch some rolling tumblers. The water was a deep clear turquoise. I didn't even need to see Third Bay; this was perfect.

"Well, that's enough of this kiddy stuff," Rom said. "Shall we, gents?"

Like sheep, we followed. Stupid sheep.

12. I USUALLY LIKED to think of the sea as a nurturing mother, a giver of life. But as we rounded the lava rocks that divided Second and Third Bay, as the swell transformed from manageable turquoise into blue open-water surges that exploded against the rock, I began to resonate with how Hawaiian legends described Kanaloa, the sea's ruler: a sea monster—god of death and darkness, the king of the underworld.

I trembled as I paddled.

One of my favorite verses, a song by the spirit Ariel in Shakesepare's *The Tempest*, popped into my head. It's one I've always thought illustrates the beautiful notion that, because everything is interconnected, death may be more like trading in your old rusty parts than a definitive end. Given the circumstances, however, the words failed to comfort:

> Full fathom five thy father lies;
> Of his bones are coral made;
> Those are pearls that were his eyes;
> Nothing of him that doth fade
> But doth suffer a sea-change
> Into something rich and strange

As we paddled deeper, the monsters of my childhood began to flash in my mind: rhino-like turtles as big as islands, giant squid with tentacles the size of redwoods, krakens and leviathans. I heard them all warning me, "We will kill you. Go back."

13. "IT'S A LITTLE SHIFTY," Rom said as we pushed on, meaning that the waves were breaking in different places and that we were going to have a hard time knowing where to situate without getting caught inside. "It'll be tough to line up."

While still well outside of the break point, a swell finally came through that foreshadowed things to come. The surge filled in under my board and it felt as if a great blue whale had breasted right below, lifted me high out of the water, and plunged back down.

No one else was surfing Third Bay, and because it can be difficult to feel when the current is tugging you along, we had to find markers on land to gauge our drift. Eventually, the consensus was that we could line up with a bent palm tree on shore and a rock outcropping to the south. Rom looked at us and grinned widely.

"Man," he said, "I've gotta try this."

WIZARDS AND WATER-WALKING

14. AT THE MONASTERY, we often chanted the name of Kuan-yin bodhisattva, or Avalokiteshvara, the bodhisattva of compassion. A bodhisattva is a being who has attained the wisdom to escape the endless cycle of suffering but nonetheless compassionately vows to remain in the world for the benefit of suffering beings. Reciting Kuan-yin's name in any language, many Buddhists believe, will keep you safe from harm.

Ever the skeptic, I always tried to use the Chinese chant—*"Namo Kuan-Shi-Yin Pusa"*—as a mantra alone, a concentration tool. Praying for outside intervention seemed cultish, overly religious.

But as the saying goes, there are no atheists in a foxhole. And as Rom paddled into the takeoff zone, I cried to Kuan-yin for help.

"Namo Kuan-Shi-Yin Pusa. Namo Kuan-Shi-Yin Pusa."

Rom missed the first wave—and I was glad. It growled, spitting a puff of mist out of its shadowy maw. But Rom didn't back off. He didn't hesitate. He caught the third wave of the set. And from my vantage point, behind the wave, Rom disappeared as he dropped.

And the wave's lip smacked loudly against the water.

"Namo Kuan-Shi-Yin Pusa. Namo Kuan-Shi-Yin Pusa."

15. Ryan wasn't having it. "Well, that just about does it for me," he said. "I've seen it. This place is spooking me."

All my reasoning faculties, plus the sea monsters, were telling me to paddle back with Ryan. But reason has never been my strong suit. And I guess I wanted to believe the sea monsters were just illusions, like Mara's army, that I had to see through. I also wanted to believe Rom was right: "Stories, stories," he'd said. "Every spot has stories."

It was beyond my ability level. But I believed I could do it—kind of. *Did I believe I could do it?* Rom saw me hedging. "Ah, just go for it, " he laughed. "I reckon it's the best ride this park has. Something to tell your friends back home about."

I don't know if vanity or bravery motivated me. But I nodded, swallowed the lump in my throat, and paddled in. The sets were coming about every ten minutes. And a very long ten minutes passed. I scooped clear saltwater in my hands and tried to see that it was all basically the same stuff, it was all the sea: tears, sweat, blood, crushing saltwater behemoths. I tried to pretend it was a peaceful morning on Dawn Patrol: no pressure, just me and the waves.

And maybe death wouldn't be so bad: *A sea-change. Into something rich and strange.*

16. THE HORIZON BULGED. *Kanaloa*, I thought— *death*.

I was supposed to paddle for the wave, but instead I paddled over the top, barely cresting the lip as it feathered. It sounded angry when it broke below. I would have passed on the next one, too, but Rom was shouting, "This one's yours!"

I turned my board, pointed it toward the rocks and began pumping my hands through the water. The thing began to lift, kept lifting. Up, up, up. I was looking down the line of a horizontal tornado and my board picked up speed. I didn't hesitate. My body somehow knew. I felt the split-second moment to pop, did so, and pointed right.

Then... speed. Unbelievable speed. Not walking on water. Running. Gliding. *Flying*. No separate self. No Jaimal riding. No wave about to crush me. No thought. Just the sound of thunder behind me. Just a blue wall transforming. Just—I saw the rocks coming.

I pulled out. Safe.

"This is it, man!" Rom was shouting. "We have it all to ourselves." He started whooping and hooting like a six-year-old. I sat there shaking, smiling. It seemed like my skin would start cracking from the buzz inside. And then it busted out of me. "Whooooo!" I screamed. "OH MY GOD!"

I was ready for another one. I felt like I could do anything. But oddly enough, as if Kanaloa was saying,

"Get out while I still like you," the waves started withering and the tide got too high.

After some failed attempts for a second rush, we paddled back to our bikes.

17. DURING THE NEXT MONTH, we surfed Third Bay a few more times on relatively small days like that. And each time we surfed, I saw that the *idea* of Third Bay was more scary than any actual wave itself—at least up to a point. (For those who have surfed it when it's big, I make no claims to even imagine what that's like.)

One day when Rom was working, I went alone. From the parking lot, I could make out a silhouette of a single bobbing surfer against the horizon. The sun would be setting in an hour and a half and it didn't make much sense to brave the twenty-minute paddle. But I guess I wanted to show myself that I didn't need Rom to come with me to Third Bay every time.

When I arrived, I saw the single surfer: a middle-aged man with bright green eyes and a deep scar across his forehead. His leathered skin and beat-up big-wave board made him look like he'd been drifting on ocean currents for twenty years.

I nodded, and he gave a wide grin revealing a few missing teeth.

"Small today," he said, "mostly just a drop." He pointed to the horizon. "But it'll change. You see 'em out there?"

I didn't see anything but big white clouds.

"Who?"

"Dragons."

"Sorry?"

"*Dra-gons*. Been watching 'em. Sort of a hobby."

Had we been sitting at any other of Pohoiki's breaks, I would have welcomed the man's visions. But on my first day at Third Bay without Rom, surfing with a guy having acid flashbacks was not my idea of fun. I considered paddling back, but I was tired. I decided to catch my breath for a few minutes.

"They're in the clouds—Lono," the man said, referencing the Hawaiian god who rules over storms. "That's the way they appear. Lot of messages in the clouds."

The clouds did seem unusually huge and the outer edges of the billows formed clean hard lines. The low sun was turning the backs of the billows into a velvety rose color. It was easy to see any number of mythological creatures writhing inside: dancing, fighting, mating.

At that point, a set came through with the usual ferocity. I thought the old man was too late, too deep, but at the zenith, he stood gracefully, pulling a smooth bottom turn then gliding off the back.

I still felt uneasy around the guy and I watched my mind start to make up stories—what jokes I would tell Rom the next day. But I stopped. I remembered how fun it was to make shapes out of clouds when I was little... and that reminded me of a Zen teaching that real insight comes from letting go of fixed views: assumptions that the world is a certain way. Rather than constantly spinning out a web of assumptions, Zen teaches to be with what actually *is*, moment to moment. To watch how everything changes, how everything comes into being and passes away.

And in *that* moment, the clouds did look something like dragons. It would've been an assumption to say they were dragons, but also an assumption to say they weren't.

So I tried to let my judgments dissolve. For the rest of the evening, as the leathered man and I exchanged waves, I tried to be a five-year-old in my mother's garden with a fairy-catching net. And maybe it was the lighting, or the power of suggestion, or the adrenaline that Third Bay catalyzed. But for brief moments that evening, it almost seemed like each thing around me—not just the clouds, but the stones, the trees, the wind—was a living organism.

"You have to ask permission when you come in here," the man said, paddling back toward me. "Some people don't. They get washed up on the rocks."

Bobbing on the fingertips of Kanaloa, his words carried some gravitas.

I asked permission.

Part VI
SURF NAZIS HAVE BUDDHA-NATURE TOO

The irony of it was that most of the people there considered surfing a religious experience and that their religious experience was being ruined by all the others surfing for the same reason.
—Steven Kotler

Where there are humans, you'll find flies— and buddhas.
—Kobayashi Issa

1. IN HAWAII, I saw a few fights break out. But I never had any personal collisions with the so-called "localism factor" until I came back to the mainland— or, as the Rastafarians in Hawaii call it, "Babylon."

After six months at Kalani, I figured I couldn't live in my heavenly little A-frame forever, so I moved back to California for college classes. To keep up what Rom taught me, I went to that little college town called Santa Cruz: liberal bubble of idealism and drum circles, of health-food stores that out-number Starbucks, of really good cold waves, and, as I would soon find out, angry surfers.

At first I was too tucked away to notice them. I found a quiet studio in Aptos next to a park of red-woods and lolling ferns. Fog cloaked my bedroom windows most mornings and I meditated before dawn to the sound of trickling dew. I could walk to a good beach break and to my new job at the Farm Bakery. I fell in love with a pretty Santa Cruz girl and we tried to be healthy, spiritual do-gooders: yoga classes, monthly beach clean-ups, hospice work, lots of raw vegetables. All was well in the Santa Cruzian cosmos. And I could generally avoid surfing in town where the so-called Surf Nazis roamed.

I first heard this name in my oceanography class. "That's what people call those assholes," said a surfer from L.A. who sat next to me. "And they really are

Nazis, man, I swear. They think they own the ocean. Man, L.A. was better than this."

"Really? L.A.?"

"Well, you expect it more down there. I thought northern Californians were supposed to be more friendly."

"We are."

"Not in Santa Cruz, man."

2. To be fair, angry locals exist everywhere there is a combination of two things: good waves and male surfers. Serene as our sport can be, put a bunch of testosterone-crazed men in close proximity competing for anything, even just fleeting bursts of saltwater, and there will be problems.

On the whole, I'd say Barton Lynch, the 1988 surf champ, got it right when he said that surfers are "more cocky and judgmental than any group of people in the world." And Santa Cruz surfers are known as the worst. Not that there aren't a lot of friendly surfers in Santa Cruz, but the Nazis do enough heckling, shouting, and beating to eclipse the others.

I suppose it's not their fault. Aside from the cold water—usually about fifty-five degrees—it would be hard to *design* a better surf locale than Santa Cruz. The entire bay faces south, which means the northwest winds that pound the rest of northern California blow offshore in Santa Cruz and keep the waves tidy almost every day, year-round. Santa Cruz is open to gentle south swells all summer. And in winter, the powerful northern swells that overfill many north-facing breaks get parceled, manicured, and groomed as they bend into the Monterey Bay and collide with Santa Cruz's sedimentary reefs. When all the right factors combine, it can be a stunning sight.

At some point long, long ago in the dark ages of surfing—before the invention of the wetsuit—Santa

Cruz surfers were a brazen, chill-tolerant few with the pristine sanctuary to themselves. But Jack O'Neill changed everything. In 1952, he invented the wetsuit and opened his first real surf shop in Santa Cruz shortly after. The wetsuit* allowed even old ladies, small children, and wimpy Buddhists onto the waves; Santa Cruz transformed from hippie town with a few polar bear club surfers to hippie town with a surf-driven economy. Today, the area seems to have more surf shops than it does gas stations. And from Sunset Beach to Scott's Creek, when the surf is good, thousands of wet-suited surfers descend on the sea and fill every nook and cove, competing for anything that ripples, refracts, or gurgles.

It's still a great place to be a surfer. But you have to feel a little bad for the born-and-bred Santa Cruz surfers, whose solitary Eden has been opened wide to every over-eager UC Santa Cruz student, every Silicon Valley drudge fending off a mid-life crisis, and every newly christened surfer coming back from six months in Hawaii and trying to beat culture shock.

So, of course they try to defend their turf—not that that justifies some of their actions. But everything is created by causes and conditions.

* For which, Mr. O'Neill, I am very grateful.

3. I FINALLY WITNESSED genuine Surf Nazi rage at a well-populated town spot called the Hook. It was a crowded, small day, and there was much more jockeying for space than surfing going on. But it was also sunny. The air was clear. And everyone who wasn't getting waves—all but about seven guys—probably figured just sitting in the water was still better than whatever else they had to do.

After an hour or so, I watched three grinning boys paddle out with their shiny new gear, jabbering about girls in their dorm or something. They weren't terrible surfers. They just had terrible judgment. They paddled directly to the wrong take-off point and dropped in on the wrong guy, a stocky blonde with a chin like Arnold Schwarzenegger.

"What the fuck are you doing?" the Arnold-chin guy yelled.

"Surfing," the boy replied.

It was a brave response. But the wrong one. Within minutes, the boys were slipping on seaweed and ducking hurled rocks. The boys darted back into their SUV, not even bothering to change out of their wetsuits.

Arnold-chin and his friends were proud of themselves. In their minds, I imagine, they were doing their duty: protecting their pristine shores. The three of them laughed about it for a good fifteen minutes— "They were so fucking scared"—and on and on.

Then they went back to their conversation about the previous night's exploits.

"I was sooo wasted. Keyed. Seriously."

"I know, dude, how many times did you use the N-word?"

"About thirty. But I don't mean it like that, man."

Perhaps they had earned the name Nazis for a reason. Anyway, I didn't want to deal with them. So I surfed conservatively, smiled a lot and apologized profusely whenever I came close to breaking a taboo.

It worked for a long time. But then one day, I was in downtown Santa Cruz during a big winter swell. Normally, I'd have headed to one of the more secluded coves up north, but I only had ninety minutes before class.

So I drove down to Santa Cruz's most famous and crowded spot: Steamer Lane.

4. THE LANE BECAME FAMOUS in the '60s as a good training spot for Makaha and Sunset and other big-wave Hawaiian surf spots. It has since become so "localized" that even the parking lot is divided between locals and non-locals. In other words, before you even touch the water, you know where you stand in the pecking order. And because the wave breaks in perfect view from the Santa Cruz surf museum and lighthouse, a popular tourist lookout, the Lane is like a surf auditorium built for show-offs. It breeds the worst in localism and the best in surfing acrobatics. Not surprisingly, the two often go together.

I'd surfed the Lane a handful of times and I knew where I stood. I parked in the tourist lot and walked to the lighthouse to have a look. The railing on the cliff was brimming with families flashing cameras, students playing Frisbee, and mobs of surfers, all of them gawking.

"OH! MY! GOD!" I heard someone shout. And then I saw it. In the surf slang of the moment, the Lane was "going off": ten-foot faces backlit by a warm sun unwrapped across the inlet like a magazine cover. I'd heard the Lane got good. But I had had no idea it could do this.

Dozens of surfers spread out in tight-knit groups like little islands. The best surfers waited in a pack at the most dangerous spot behind the jutting cliff. I watched a big set come in. The surfer furthest behind the cliff caught it, streamed down the face, narrowly missing the cliff's edge as the wall of water collided with the sediment and shot white spume twenty-five feet vertically.

"Oohhh," the tourists cooed.

"Sick," said the surfer next to me. "So critical."

5. I GRABBED MY BOARD and climbed quickly down the cement steps into the water. On a sign near the entrance, someone had written, "You're not a local until you've lived in Santa Cruz for seven years."

Charming. Just six years and eight months to go.

I paddled to middle point, a peak safely away from the rocks. And despite the crowd, surprising myself, I got a few very good rides; the waves were setting up in a predictable line, almost like—I hate to say it—a surfing video game. Plenty of room to carve around on the face, time to think about your next snap.

A few professionals (and lots of aspiring professionals) were out in the lineup. Everyone, even the women, seemed to be doing their best alpha-male impersonation: jaw thrust forward, eyes steely, shoulders back, no smiles. Only the good old boys were talking at all, cracking inside jokes to let everyone know that they did indeed own this wave (in case we somehow forgot).

It was a quintessential Santa Cruz day. Between waves, I watched in envy as guys like Darryl Virostko, known as Flea, pulled floaters and aerial maneuvers like his board was an extension of his body. He was like a human-board hybrid. A herd of seals was sunning on a nearby rock. Purple and yellow flowers bloomed like fireworks. The cliffs twinkled like new sandpaper.

Peter, a guy I knew from English class, was out at middle point, too. He surfed the Lane regularly and said he'd never seen it so good. "This is rare beauty," he said. "Santa Cruz gold."

"I think these may be the best waves I've ever ridden," I told him.

"They may be the best waves you'll ride for a long time, too. This swell's gonna be over by tomorrow. Get 'em while you can."

Middle point was plenty of fun. But after months in Hawaii, I had a chip on my shoulder. And before long, I paddled over toward the pack near the cliff. The waves were steeper over there, barreling in an almond shape as they rumbled by the cliff's edge.

I was a little nervous. I still hadn't gotten a good tube ride, ever.

The art of getting inside the wave looks easy in videos and magazines. But it's actually about as difficult as threading a needle wearing mittens and a blindfold. Making it out of the tube was the hardest part for me. Almost every time I'd made it in, the wave had swallowed.

I knew I had to prove myself if I was going to sit behind the cliff and get any respect. And again, I got unbelievably lucky. On the first wave I paddled into, as I passed the cliff, the lip leapt outward like it was reaching for shore. I ducked, pressed my body close to the face, and a thin sheath of water just fell over my shoulder. It was like ducking behind a waterfall, like breathing underwater, like being shot through the barrel of a shotgun. It was all of this, and also like nothing else. It was *my first real tube*. I wasn't deep inside the hollow section, but I was definitely in the shade of the lip, enough for the periscope vision I'd been dreaming about.

I heard hoots from the crowd before the wave spat me out in a burst.

6. I FELT LIKE I'D JUST WON THE LOTTERY. I wanted to scream to the tourists: "I know what it feels like, suckers!" But one never breaks stoic coolness at a spot like the Lane. Never. So I acted the part—just one of the boys.

But as Kurt Vonnegut Jr. once wrote, "We are what we pretend to be, so we must be careful what we pretend to be." I paddled back with fierce confidence: back arched, stare forward. I figured everyone had seen my wave and that everyone would gladly give me waves the rest of the evening. I paddled deeper into the pack and waited.

But then I made a slight faux pas. Okay, a big one. On my next wave, I didn't even look to see if anyone was dropping in before me. I just rode, like Tupac, nothing but open wave ahead—pure freedom. And as I rode—*yeah! yeah!*—I heard a voice: "HO-HO-HO! HO-HO-HO!" Unfortunately this was not a festive greeting. This meant in surf-speak: "Get the hell out of my way, now!"*

* I have no idea which surfer started saying "HO" to signal that the wave is already taken. But it seems to be used all over the world now. I know one surfer who has tacked on a "Merry Christmas" when the other surfer gets off the wave. And unrelatedly, but in an interesting coincidence, repeatedly chanting "Ho" is also what Zen monks in Japan intone on their begging rounds—it's the Japanese word for "Dharma."

I looked back to see a surfer in a bright red wetsuit. And no one wears a bright red wetsuit unless they really want to be noticed. He was barreling down the line right toward me, screaming now: "HO! HO!"

Technically, it was his wave. And I tried to follow etiquette and pop off the back of the wave. But for some reason, when I did that I didn't bring my board. I jumped off, diving over the lip. Thus, *I* was safely out of the way, but my board was not. And it tripped him. I was all set with my overdone apology when I heard him scream. "Errrggghhhmotherfucker!" *Oh man.* He was angry, very angry. He paddled toward me spewing words in what almost sounded like fast-forward.

"Whatthefuckareyoudoingfuckingidiotmotherfuckinfaggothomo*ERRGGHH*!"

"I'm really sorry," I said. "I am really, really sorry! I tried to—"

"Faggotyourefuckingluckyyoudidntdingmyboard. Errrghnowgetoutand*learntofuckingsurf*."

"Hey, I said I was sorry."

"Whydontyoufuckinglooknextfuckingtimefuckingbuttpirate."

7. DESPITE HIS POOR MANNERS and slurred speech I felt bad. It was my fault. If I hadn't been pretending I was Kelly Slater, it wouldn't have happened. I apologized again and expected the incident would be over. I wasn't going to get out like he wanted me to. He didn't look older than twenty-one and he wasn't even a great surfer. Besides, everyone gets dropped in on from time-to-time. It happened a thousand times a day at Steamer Lane. He would let it go.

But for the next *twenty minutes*, the red-suited bandit and his friend, a guy in a bright blue suit and a fluorescent orange top, taunted me with more homophobic obscenities and fast-forward surf slang.

It was really annoying.

And I wasn't going to fight them. For one thing, judging from their crew cuts, bright suits, and political incorrectness, I figured they probably had older brothers with black monster trucks waiting in the parking lot to run over Buddhist surfers. Secondly, I don't think I could effectively hold my own against an aggressive *starfish* if I wanted to. And thirdly, back at the monastery I took a lifelong vow against killing (and fighting) that I'd upheld thus far—with the exception of a few mosquitoes, which I regret. And since I'd broken most of the other vows many times over, I wanted to maintain at least one. I tried to ignore them:

"Deedadeee. Happy thoughts, happy thoughts."

But after the tenth time the red-suited surfer yelled "faggot" at me, I began to lose my patience. Perhaps if he'd been a little bit more creative—"Hey sea horse, are you pregnant?" "Hey hippo mouth"—I would've taken it in stride. But *faggot*? It was as if these guys had been stuck in a time warp—Miami Beach, 1985—and had suddenly beamed down to Steamer Lane just to test my patience.

I paddled away, but I couldn't surf at all well. My chest began to tighten. My ribs compressed. I felt nauseous. I was getting... angry. And that was not good. Good Buddhists don't get angry, I told myself (unhelpfully). And every time I looked at their bright suits, the anger grew. And every time the anger grew, I got angry at myself for getting angry. Suddenly, on a beautiful day with the best surf of the year, nothing felt right.

The water was cold. My hands were clammy. I started hating everyone, all the stupid surfers, all the ridiculous followers who just wanted a cool surfer identity, which was the only reason they were out.

Unlike me—obviously the only soul surfer left— they were obstacles. Flotsam.

8. SHANTIDEVA, a famous Indian Buddhist philosopher in the eighth century, said that a single moment of anger can destroy eons of good karma. The law of karma, of course, is the causal notion that wholesome deeds always yield wholesome results and unwholesome deeds inevitably lead to unwholesome results. What you reap is what you sow, basically.

Me, I didn't quite believe that karma worked so straightforwardly just then. But anyway, I figured I should heed Shantideva's warning and not act out my anger. Plus, I didn't think I had much good karma to spare. I'd only just started being an official do-gooder in that year. And in all honesty, the beach clean-ups were more of a way to spend time with my girlfriend, who seemed to never have enough time to see me because she was always saving the earth.

So I told myself, "I need to handle this peacefully. I *meditate*. I'm spiritual. The red-suited demon is just a test. Remember Siddhartha, remember Mara."

I dug deep into my Buddhist training.

I tried to analyze the anger. Hui-neng, the Sixth Ancestor of Zen, said of the enlightened mind: "The ear hears sounds but the mind doesn't move." I'd heard the sounds ("hey faggot"), judged them, and reacted by tensing up. That reaction was based on my perception of a fixed self—a self I felt was currently under threat and in need of defending—my memory patterns, and cultural programming, and this reaction was the proximal thing causing me to suffer. Sure, the guy was a bit uncouth. But he wasn't shoving my own burning anger down my throat. The anger was coming from inside *me*. In principle, I had a choice.

Then I recalled that the Buddha said that the causes of anger were frustrated desire or wounded pride. I didn't want to admit it, but obviously my pride had been wounded, a lot. "Learn to surf," the jerk in red had said. In the space of a wave, I'd gone—in my own mind—from one of the best surfers at the Lane, to the worst. And really, I was more angry about that than anything.

I took a deep breath and recited my little Buddhist catchphrases: "Just surf, Jaimal. Present moment. Everything passes. Nothing permanent."

It helped. But I still felt queasy and still kind of wanted that red-suited devil-child to faceplant in the cliff.

So I moved on to stage two: generate compassion. I silently recited the Metta Sutra, the Buddha's discourse on loving-kindness: "Even as a mother protects with her life her child, her only child, so with a boundless heart should one cherish all living beings." I tried to see the brightly colored homophobes as fellow humans who were in the same boat of suffering, who wanted to be happy, just like me, who wanted good waves, just like me. But I couldn't do it.

SURF NAZIS HAVE BUDDHA-NATURE TOO

I found myself visualizing throwing spiny purple sea urchins at their heads, each one lodging itself in their stupid little faces.

9. SO WHAT ABOUT SOMETHING MORE HUMAN, I thought, something witty? What would Dave Chapelle say? Or Mr. Miyagi? No. No. I racked my brain for something that would teach these boys *a lesson*. I remembered that surf writer Dan Duane (one of my writing heroes) had a similar encounter with a teenager at Steamer Lane and, in *his* book, he'd said to the kid, "I could have an Uzi in my car." You know, just to shake the kid up a little. That was pretty clever. Yeah, I'd tell these guys *I had an Uzi*—oh, who was I kidding? If anyone had an Uzi, it was their older brothers with the freaking monster trucks.

The whole situation sucked.

I couldn't calm down. And I couldn't surf. And I couldn't say anything to them. And I obviously wasn't as spiritually evolved as I'd imagined. And I was probably repressing my anger into a spiky little bomb that would erupt years from now and turn me into a serial killer who preyed on people wearing red.

I tried to catch a wave and fell. The red-suited devil saw me fall and yelled again, "Faggot!"

Man, he was a little shit. But I tried to fake it, play it cool. I met eyes with him a couple times, grinned and raised my eyebrows as if to say, you're not bothering me so you might as well give up. But he knew he was bothering me. He splashed me. "Isaidgohome-stupidfaggotidiothomoyou'renotwelcomehereerrrgghhh-gothefuckhome."

And then, something strange happened, something cool. Well, first I threw more make-believe sea urchins at his head. But *then* something cool happened.

As he continued shouting, I watched his face in more detail. When he yelled, it contorted and tightened; it reminded me of a sick pig. The veins in his throat bulged. And it was obvious when I looked closely: the red-suited devil was not having a good time. In fact, he appeared to be in just as much pain as I was, and his pain was self-inflicted, just like mine. And he just couldn't let go, just like I couldn't— despite all my spiritual training.

We were both holding on to this *thing*, this monster between us. And now that I saw it, I could almost feel it hovering there, tangible. It was wrapping its stickiness around our throats—and we were helping it. We were grabbing on to it tightly, believing it was part of us. But it wasn't. It was a thing we'd each created. It was a bad wave we'd caught and it had closed out and was holding us down. All we needed to do was *let it pass*. All we needed to do was stop grabbing at it.

And when I saw this, I did let go—a little. And then a little more. I let myself breath more naturally. And when I did this, I even felt kind of bad for the guy. And when I felt kind of bad for the guy, as if on cue, he and his buddy paddled in. As they walked up the steps, they continued shouting nonsense. The red-suited kid even stood on the cliff for a few minutes flailing his arms and screaming obscenities that I couldn't even hear. I had to give him points for perseverance, but silhouetted against the sky, he just looked like he was having a seizure.

"What's up that guy's ass?" said Peter, who'd been surfing middle point the whole time and hadn't heard the incident.

"I dropped in on him. But he seems to be more angry at life in general."

"Yeah. Apparently. Must have a hell of a home life. What's he saying?"

"No idea."

We laughed about it a little, about the ridiculousness of fighting while playing in the waves, and the knot in my chest started to untie. I was still a little mad, but more at myself than at the kid. The red-suited guy seemed like a caricature of anger.

Or maybe a bodhisattva who'd come to compassionately demonstrate what can happen without anger management skills.

10. A BURLY SAMURAI once came to a Zen master and asked the master, "Sensei, please teach me the difference between heaven and hell."

"Why would I give an uncouth cretin like you such a high teaching," the Zen master said, in apparent disgust. "You're a worm. You're less than a worm. You're a stupid samurai."

Samurai were never treated this way in ancient Japan and the samurai grew instantly enraged. His eyes bulged and he raised his shiny sword, ready to slice the little monk in two.

But the Zen master didn't flinch. (They never do.) He said to the samurai, calmly, "That, Samurai, is hell."

Suddenly, understanding the teaching, realizing that he was about to kill a holy man because of his own pride, the samurai's eyes filled with tears. He put his sword down and his palms together in reverence. He bowed deeply.

"And that," said the master, "is heaven."

11. LOOKING BACK OVER THE WATER, I noticed it was actually a fabulous day. The sun, now a dark orange, was beginning to sink behind the cliff. The water was turning from a jade green to an oily black flecked with points of light. Brown pelicans, with their pterodactyl-like wingspans, skimmed the water, reading the wave lines better than any of us. A spotted harbor seal near the cliff raised its whiskered head above water and glanced around before diving back down.

I breathed the cold salt air in deeply.

Heaven.

Part VII
WANTED: ONE GURU, APPLY WITHIN

The Supreme Way by nature is all embracing, not easy, not difficult. But quibbling and hesitating, the more you hurry, the slower you go.
—Seng-Tsan

Whether you believe in God or not does not matter so much, whether you believe in Buddha or not does not matter so much. You must lead a good life.
—The Dalai Lama

True religion is real living; living with all one's soul, with all one's goodness and righteousness.
—Albert Einstein

1. ZEN IS ONLY ONE BRANCH of many in Buddhism. Another is called Pure Land and I used to think it was, frankly, really dumb.

Pure Land Buddhism is structured around reciting Amitabha Buddha's name in order to be reborn in his Western Pure Land (a heaven realm somewhere in the western part of the universe).

Unlike the Christian heaven, the Pure Land is not the end-all-be-all heaven. It's just a really nice stopover on your way to ending suffering and realizing full buddhahood, kind of a five-star meditation center.

The Pure Land sounds great. Amitabha's body is made of golden light. People are born from lotus blossoms. Sweet sounds trickle like dew from flower petals and multi-colored birds fly around. Everything is made of lapis lazuli and precious gems. But the real perk is that everything, every little sound and sight, reminds you of the Buddha's teaching. Everything speaks Dharma, ultimate truth.

At the monastery, we recited the Pure Land sutra every morning and Aran and I sometimes rolled our eyes when it came around. We considered ourselves intelligent Zen practitioners—skeptical Buddhists— not superstitious *Pure Landers*. Pure Land Buddhism, we concluded (without much historical knowledge), was for peasants who needed a savior; and we didn't.

So we'd recite half-heartedly, but also with what we imagined to be ultra-Zen focus.

But then one day, the Pure Land redeemed itself under our rigid Zen standards. (Almost all the different Buddhist schools eventually deconstruct themselves into something totally in tune with each other.) After we'd recited the Buddha's name time after time at the monastery, Heng Sure, the abbot, popped a little surprise in one of his evening lectures: "Actually, good effort, but there's no need to go to any other land. When your mind is pure, everything is the Pure Land. Your life right now is the Pure Land."

I can't speak for Aran, but when I heard this little twist, I started liking the Pure Land Buddhism a whole lot more. I have an active imagination and sometimes Zen was a little too simple. Staring at a white wall could be a little slow. So, without telling any of my Zen-snob buddies, I liked to pretend everything was the Pure Land, that my life was already perfect as it was.

It was fun to visualize lotus blossoms with Buddhas everywhere: popping out of sunroofs, swimming in my blueberry smoothie, picnicking on everyone's front lawn. It made my day better and I found myself reciting Amitabha Buddha's name (*Amitofo*, in Chinese) while doing my grocery shopping or strolling around town.

2. I OFTEN IMAGINED Santa Cruz was the American Pure Land—the realm in the western quadrant of the American universe—because sometimes it seemed like paradise. West Cliff Drive when the light was reflecting on the water just so, and the waves were feathering, and the roller skaters were twirling, and the students were holding **NO WAR** signs, and the Hare Krishnas were giving out chocolate, and everything was in bloom... there was something very heavenly about it.

And like Amitabha's Pure Land, lots of things in Santa Cruz reminded one to practice. Really, I wouldn't be surprised if there were a Buddha statue in every Santa Cruz home. And there seemed to be more meditation centers per capita in the area than anywhere in California. There were at least two Zen centers, a few Tibetan temples, and more yoga gurus than most towns in India.

I made the rounds. I learned some Sanskrit mantras and stood on my head for too long and projected myself into the Great Mandala. I bowed at the various gurus' feet and got their *shaktipat*, their touch of purified consciousness or whatever. I was curious.

But eventually I went back to being a somewhat jaded Zen Buddhist without a teacher. I decided that the whole guru thing wasn't for me, at least not in the formal sense. Problems with authority, I guess. But it was more than that, too. A lot of the "guru-gurus" I saw or heard seemed to have a weird hierarchical following that reminded me of a pyramid scheme, of spiritual celebrity-ism. I didn't spend enough time with any one of them to name names. But I saw enough to know that I just wasn't a guru kind of guy.

And that was a big recognition for me. When I first got into Buddhism, all I'd wanted was an old rickety Zen master to whack me with a stick and give me impossible koans and teach me to chop trees down with my bare hands. I had wanted the Buddhist fairy tale. I was guru-needy. (And I didn't like it when anyone suggested this might be because I wasn't close with my dad.) But in the same way that smoking too much all at once can make you want to quit, Santa Cruz seemed to cure me of my guru obsession.

And maybe that was the Western Pure Land's real teaching: If everything teaches Dharma all the time, what do you need a guru for?

3. ALL MY FAVORITE ZEN MASTERS said everyday life is the path. And since surfing was my everyday life, I sat at the ocean's feet. She always had lessons. And she didn't tithe. She didn't have a hierarchy (even if some of the other surfers did) and she didn't ask me to obey secret codes. She just ebbed and flowed, demonstrated impermanence, and slapped me around when I needed it.

So as summer turned to fall and the monarch butterflies migrated through Natural Bridges State Beach, I left my studio to be a full-time ocean devotee. I parked my van along West Cliff and slept on the cold beach and didn't care that I went to class with sand in my hair. I surfed and surfed and surfed and sat in cafes and drank lots of tea and meditated in the verdant hills.

It was kind of fun. For a while.

Eventually, of course, living in a van in Santa Cruz and puppy-dogging after a girl who never had enough time for me stopped working for me. I really missed hot showers. So I moved away, to Berkeley, and took classes at Cal and eventually fell in love with a responsible girl.

But I hated *driving* to the surf. I really hated it. I began to go completely insane and no amount of meditating could cure it. My girlfriend was wondering if I had some strange illness. I *needed* to get back to the sea, I told her. But I didn't want to go back to Santa

Cruz, to the Surf Nazis and cold water and the gurus. I'd had enough of that Pure Land.

So I used the old fallback. I executed my familiar escape routine once again: one-way ticket to Hawaii, upheaval with loved ones, deciding which island to go to, blah blah blah. You've heard it.

And I know you think I was just running away (again). Hell, even I thought I was just running away. But I figured it was okay. I mean, I was making progress, right? This time my trip had a *responsible* edge. I applied to the University of Hawaii at Hilo— yes, possibly the worst-ranked university in the country, but *still* a university—as a religious studies major.

4. AFTER MY TIME living in the monastery, I could write Eastern philosophy essays with my eyes closed—which meant ample time for surfing, and that's what mattered.

Surfing really, *really* mattered.

Having been away from warm water for two years, on this trip I got fanatical. I woke at five AM to check the waves. I surfed twice a day. My back muscles turned to rocks and my nose peeled in perpetuity. When there wasn't surf, I ran and lifted weights and swam long distances to stay fit. I daydreamed about waves. I nightdreamed about waves. When I meditated, I visualized myself tucking into waves, endless barrels—my new version of Zen emptiness.

I didn't realize how much I was obsessing until Aran, with whom I usually had deep conversations about love and philosophy and politics, called me one night from California. He told me about everything going on in his life and wanted to know about mine.

"Uh, I don't know," I found myself saying. I honestly couldn't think of anything I was doing but surfing. No deep thoughts. No life outside of the weather patterns.

"Well, tell me about surfing," he said.

"Well, I do it a lot."

My mind was saltwater.

I drifted further from formal Buddhist practice and everything else that didn't peel or tube or pitch. My grades suffered. I still sat my daily zazen session. But it became shorter and shorter until it almost wasn't there. Which was okay with me. I saw "merging with the waves" as my new practice. Surfing was becoming my official religion.

It's not that I was giving up on Zen. But I saw surfing as the best Zen practice. By this point, I'd done weeks and weeks of formal Zen retreats in lots of different monasteries. I didn't think I was any hotshot meditator, but I'd experienced some interesting meditative states—but so what?

And after all that, it still seemed to me that the mind brought forth while surfing a wave was as close as I'd come to Zen. The great ancestor Sengcan described the Zen mind by saying that the subject disappears without objects, objects vanish without a subject. And centuries later in Japan, Master Dogen talked of dropping off of one's body and mind, and the body and mind of others. Riding a wave, this happened naturally. The wave demanded such hyperfocus, there wasn't room for judging. On a steep, hollow wave, there wasn't even time to differentiate between one's body and the wave. There was only *this* and *this* and *this*. Just power and presence.

And, I thought, if I could only hold that focus when the wave ended, I would be a Buddha. But I

5. WHEN THERE WEREN'T WAVES IN HILO, or when it was raining too hard to see them, my friends and I would go to impossible lengths to find surf. We drove and hiked down every dirt road and path on the island. We skipped class and camped in deserted valleys and flew to other islands and paddled to distant reefs. In the beginning, it was fun even when there weren't waves. We were seeing sights—living the dream. Surfing videos had assured us that the endless hunt for perfect waves was the best life anyone could live. And we were *doing it.*

But I was also slowly beginning to question whether it was the best life. The more I obsessed with "getting good" at surfing, the more I noticed myself getting frustrated with mediocre waves and genuinely pissed off when the ocean was flat. Surfing was my religion, my one true love. But at the same time, it was slowly becoming an unwholesome relationship with all kinds of unhealthy expectations and needs.

The Buddha talked a lot about not attaching to the good stuff and not running from the bad stuff. Suffering, he said, arises from the mind's incessant attraction and aversion. He wasn't recommending people abandon their commonsense attraction and aversion. Putting your hand in fire hurts for a reason. Eating healthful food feels right for a reason. But the Buddha encouraged cultivating a more even-keeled mind.

6. I IMMERSED MYSELF deeper in surfing, deeper in the waves. For a few months there, I was surfing better than I ever have. My best friend at the time was an insanely good athlete named Tim. He grew up in Hawaii and was a sponsored bodyboarder, one of the best on the island. He pushed me to ride waves I never would have and took me to all the famous breaks on Oahu: Pipeline, Backdoor, Off the Wall.

Around campus, I even developed a minor reputation as a good surfer. "Dude, I saw you pull that snap the other day," a stranger at a party told me one night. "You really rip. I just wanted to give you props."

"Um, thanks," I said.

But then other people told me. And it was hard to believe. Having started surfing later than most, I never thought I'd impress even my own mom. But apparently my hard work was paying off.

And then came my downfall, running up to me in a yellow bikini, eyelashes batting. The cute surfer girl I had a crush on, Emily, was saying, "Jaimal, I saw you out there. Maybe you should start competing."

That's when my mind warped.

7. IN MY MIND, I started seeing myself on the cover of *Surfer* magazine, women fawning, cameras flashing. Result: I gradually started becoming the thing I most despised.

It started with me seeing myself as having some divine right to waves. I was still a small fish in a big pond of incredibly skilled surfers. I still knew my place (almost). But I began to see the beginners as somehow *undeserving* of waves. Sometimes, much as I hate to admit it, I didn't even like going out with my friends from school who were still learning. They embarrassed me. My *reputation* was at stake.

My attitude was trickling into my life outside the water, too. I found myself doing things I never would've done before. I caught myself in little lies. I got in a screaming match with one of my best friends over money. And the weirdest part was, I could even observe the process happening. Worse still: I didn't care.

Then one day I snapped. It was a sunny day at Honoli'i and there were tons of waves, more than enough for every surfer to get dozens. I had surfed plenty, but I still wanted more. And that was when some oblivious tourist—looking much like I once looked in those first days on Maui—dropped in right in front of me and fell, ruining a very nice wave, *my* wave.

This had happened a hundred times before and I'd never cared much. "No worries," I usually said, and paddled on. But this time, I lost it. The words just spilled out of me. "Watch where the fuck you're going," I growled. I startled even myself.

The kid looked terrified. "Sorry, man," he said. "I'm so sorry. I didn't see you."

I looked back at him—teenager, not even with any tan yet. He had the same exact look I'd had at sixteen: innocence, excitement, fear.

And that's when it hit me. I'd really gone too far. I was becoming a Surf Nazi, an extremist. I paddled over to the kid. "Look, don't worry about that fall," I told him. "Sorry I flipped. I was just worried I'd hit you."

He looked relieved. "No, that's alright. It was my bad."

I felt like such a jerk, like I wasn't any better than the Surf Nazis who I found so difficult to bear. The whole reason I'd started surfing was to find a life that was free.

Surfing was my religion—but in my confusion I was twisting it into something unrecognizable, mistaking the method for the goal, the means for the end.

I guess it happens all the time, to religious fanatics of all stripes.

8. THE BUDDHA UNDERSTOOD this problem of attaching to methodology, even though he also took great care to hone the methodology he did teach. He warned his students about engaging in unproductive practices that were all the rage in India at the time: rubbing your body in ash, worshiping fire, having sex with skulls. (I'm not sure how popular that last bit was, but it was popular enough to make it into the Buddhist rulebook.) But then he went further: He said even his own teachings were not to be taken as Ultimate Truth. He asked his students not to worship him like a god or make statues of him. He said that his teachings, to borrow a Zen phrase from centuries later, were merely a finger pointing at the moon, not the thing itself.

He also compared his teachings to a raft. The raft could be employed to cross the river of delusion and suffering. But once that shore was reached, the teachings had to be let go of. It would be foolish, he said, for someone to reach the opposite shore—of enlightenment, of freedom from suffering—and still carry the raft around on his head.

I knew very well I wasn't enlightened. And the day I screamed at the kid, I finally understood that I was carrying my surfboard around on my head and it wasn't getting me any closer to freedom. In fact, it seemed to be making me into an asshole.

So I let go a little. I surfed once a day instead of twice. I got my grades back up. I even did my own week-long silent retreat up in a little cabin on the volcano. And I got a job.

And amid all my studies of world religions, each with its own strengths and pitfalls, I saw that Buddhism, though it too had its flaws, was still a pretty good raft, at least for me. If I could get a little better at steering it.

But I still didn't want a guru.

9. NATURALLY, A GURU SHOWED UP.

He didn't come as I imagined he might. I wasn't climbing up a misty mountain. And he wasn't a fat old Zen master, or a Shaolin monk who could balance on a pin, or a hundred-and-ten-year-old yogi who could see the future.

His name was Lambert.

And he was a Hawaiian insurance agent who spent most of his day watching television. He had a passion for three things: poke (a kind of Hawaiian salad made out of raw fish, pronounced "po-kay," by the way), detective stories, and—surprisingly enough—church.

I admit that Lambert was a strange sort of guru. He didn't know anything about Buddhism. Or want to. Lambert actually thought Buddhism was kind of weird.

"I just really love Jesus," he told me one day when we were talking religion.

"Me too," I said.

"Then why are you a Buddhist?"

"I can't be a Buddhist who loves Jesus?"

"Uh, I guess. Well, I don't know. I don't see why not. But I think that makes you a Christian who likes Buddhism."

"Fine with me. But you're just trying to convert me. I mean, maybe you're a Christian who loves the Buddha and you don't even know it."

"Yeah, but I don't need to find out. I'm fine with just Jesus."

"Suit yourself. But how do you know Jesus wasn't a buddha?"

"Because he was God. I thought you said Buddha wasn't a god."

"You might have a point there. But I think it's primarily a vocabulary problem."

"You're weird."

"*You're* weird."

At first I couldn't see Lambert's teaching. I thought I was teaching Lambert. I told him about all the very profound things I learned in my religious studies classes. And since Lambert was a Christian, and I had to read the Bible a lot for class, I read Lambert the Bible almost everyday. Usually, he'd just fall asleep.

"Man, this is *your* religion and *you're* sleeping," I'd say. "Have a little respect."

"I'm just taking it in on a very deep level," Lambert muttered dreamily.

But most striking was this: we laughed a lot. And I soon learned that that was Lambert's main teaching. He always had bad jokes. And when he wasn't dropping those on me, he was making fun of me for being a vegetarian, which seemed to be an endless source of entertainment for him. He couldn't believe anyone could live without poke and beef.

"You're not going to live very long if you don't eat meat," Lambert told me all the time.

"Well, I'm doing a little better than you are, Mr. Carnivore."

"Ha ha. Very funny."

This wasn't a very good joke, actually. And I never would've said it if Lambert didn't have an incredibly good sense of humor. Lambert was the biggest optimist ever; that was his other teaching. Because considering his condition, it was amazing Lambert could even smile.

Lambert couldn't even get out of bed.

He could barely move.

10. LAMBERT HAD A RARE SICKNESS called neurofibromatosis—Elephant Man's disease. He had gotten bouts of it through his teens and twenties and he'd beaten them, somehow. But the most recent one had nearly paralyzed him.

I'd like to say I volunteered to take care of Lambert. But I met him because I needed some money and responded to a job posting for a caregiver position that also included free rent. Lambert and I hit it off right away. Suddenly I was Lambert's roommate and caregiver.

At first, I thought it would be nice just to help the guy out and save some money. I felt rather proud of myself for being a do-gooder again: *Saving Lambert*. I could almost picture the movie. What a hero I was. But after a couple weeks, it became clear that movie really would have to be called *Saving Jaimal*.

Lambert had been a handsome competitive athlete in his youth, a swimmer who was great at science and math. He had strong Hawaiian bones and huge shiny black eyes and a big sincere smile. But the disease ruined his body. It made his bones swell up. His skull got lopsided. His elbows bulged. His fingers were stuck in a half fist. He couldn't be left alone even briefly or it was likely that his lungs would fill up with fluid and he'd drown in his own mucus.

I admit that taking care of him was sort of painful at first. For one, I missed out on some of the best surf sessions of the winter. Plus, I was always tired because Lambert needed fluid sucked out of his lungs with a special machine every few hours, so I never slept more than a few hours at a time. When I did sleep, I was on the floor next to his bed so I could wake up to do the lung clearing.

But the more time I spent with Lambert, the more I liked being with him and didn't mind missing the surf, didn't mind the intimately mundane parts of the job: stretching Lambert's legs, bathing him, emptying the bed pan, cooking for him. Lambert was always upbeat and I could never maintain an emotional slump around him. Not even I could keep sulking when a paralyzed man with a fatal disease was telling jokes. It was free therapy.

Lambert's family almost never came to visit him. But he didn't complain—ever. His main social interaction was with his caregivers. But his caregivers all seemed to linger when they came to visit. They didn't want to leave. I guess they knew they were going to have to go care for a bunch of bitter patients who were angry about everything, and understandably so: most of them were dying.

Lambert was dying, too. But he didn't take it out on those around him. He never got mad at me when I messed something up—which as you might imagine happened all the time.

And that is why he's still my guru. His life is a perfect teaching. It doesn't need any clever words. The way he just abided in his life exactly as it was. This was a perfect demonstration of the core truth of the Buddha's teaching: true contentment does not come from external circumstances.

From a whole year of frantic searching for perfect waves, fanatically living my surf-religion dream, Lambert's teaching was the one lesson that really stayed with me.

So: Thank you Lambert.*

---

*P.S. Lambert, I'm sorry I haven't written. Also, I know you don't need it, but I can't help reciting Amitabha Buddha's name for you once in a while. So if you see a big golden Buddha, don't freak out. I'm betting he and Jesus know each other.

Part VIII
PADDLING OUT

I think of all the places I've been,
Chasing from one famous spot to another.
Who would guess I'd end up under a pine tree,
Clasping my knees in the whispering cold?
—Han-Shan

Aia ke ola i ka hana.
Life is in the laboring.
—Hawaiian proverb

1. MY MOM IS A CAREER COUNSELOR with a motto: *Follow your bliss*. Obviously she didn't invent that saying, but growing up I heard it mainly from her. And I guess I have tried to do it—that's why I've spent a good deal of my life surfing and meditating.

My final semester of college, I took a break from surfing. I went to India and spent four months in the Himalayas, doing meditation retreats and teaching Tibetan monks English. I sent back a couple essays on Buddhism, but I'm convinced only UH Hilo would've given credit for such a lollygagging trip.

When the diplomas were finally handed out, I realized I'd been to five different universities and community colleges and yet I felt like I'd never actually "been to college"—impressive, I guess. In a way. Immediately following graduation, I moved into my cousin's basement in San Francisco near Ocean Beach to resume my life as a surf bum. The basement received scant light and it often smelled like stale beer from my cousin's parties. But good surf waited just down the street. And he also let me stay there rent-free. Which was a good thing.

Because in all my bliss-following I've also learned something else—

My bliss doesn't pay too well.

2. I COULDN'T REALLY COMPLAIN. But there were a few little problems. First, as usual, I was broke. Second, now that I had a B.A., people (my family, for starters) were giving me the impression they thought I should get a real job. And third, I didn't *want* a real job.

Most surfers don't want real jobs, at least not full-time ones. People think we're lazy—but that's not really it. After all, it's a time-consuming business and kind of a lot of work to know when the surf will be good, to get there, and to be ready to ride it.

I had pretty much resolved to avoid real jobs for my whole life. But now that I was old—twenty-three—I was beginning to wonder if I might need one: not just now, but you know, someday.

I did find a part-time job as a barista in downtown San Francisco; and I was getting really good at making the thick foam with the little leafy designs. And I liked café work. But I had a hunch it wasn't what I wanted to do the rest of my life.

Then one day, an insight came.

And yes—of course—it happened when I was surfing.

3. I WAS PADDLING through the impact zone at Ocean Beach. Ocean Beach is widely known to have one of the hardest paddle-outs in the world. I've watched professional surfers try to make it out on big days and get sent back to the beach whimpering. There are few, if any, channels and the currents pouring in and out of the San Francisco Bay can reach seven knots, sweeping surfers up and down like driftwood on rapids. People drown there every year.

On this particular day, the waves were like endless frothy barricades. I'd been paddling for twenty minutes and I still wasn't outside. I pushed and pumped and heaved and whined. The sea punched and kicked and jammed sand down my throat. And in the midst of this abuse, I realized how much I loved surfing.

I loved the actual riding of the wave, of course. But I also loved the challenge of the paddle.

It wasn't always like that. And maybe I was just happy to be back in the water after living in India for months. Or maybe my mind was more accepting after hanging with all the ultra-happy Tibetan monks. But the more I thought about it, the more I realized every surfer has to like paddling, at least a little.

This was because extremely little of each surf session is spent actually standing up on your surfboard on a wave—maybe one percent—so if you're looking to have a good time it's essential to find a way to enjoy paddling, or at least good-naturedly bear it. And in that way, I thought, surfing is kind of a good metaphor for the rest of life.

The extremely good stuff—chocolate and great sex and weddings and hilarious jokes—fills a minute portion of an adult lifespan.

The rest of life is the paddling: work, paying bills, flossing, getting sick, dying.

I started to entertain the thought that maybe I could start to deal better with that kind of paddling too.

7. THE BUDDHA SAID something like this in his first speech after his awakening. His very first noble truth was "Life is suffering." And he encouraged all his students to reflect on this concept frequently:

> I am of the nature to age;
>> I have not gone beyond aging.
> I am of the nature to sicken;
>> I have not gone beyond sickness.
> I am of the nature to die;
>> I have not gone beyond dying.
> All that is mine, beloved and pleasing,
>> will become otherwise, will be
>> separated from me.

I guess the Buddha sounds like a bit of a downer here. But I think he was just a realist. And he was trying to get his followers to see that every moment alive is precious, in part precisely because it is fleeting. The Buddha didn't deny that there were great joys in life. But he said that as long as we humans function in our same old habituated, judging minds with their infinite preferences, much of life, even the good parts, will continue to be a cycle of struggle and pain: samsara. I like to compare the samsaric mind to a surfer who is out on the perfect day but can't settle down and enjoy it because there are too many good waves that he can't get to in time. So he paddles up and down frantically, missing most of the best waves, and getting more frustrated as he goes. The Buddha spent some forty years teaching people how to get out of that situation.

He gave all kinds of remedies, methods, and tools for doing so, meditation only being one of them. Another of those tools was home-leaving—becoming a monk, a renunciate—and getting out of the rat race altogether. Then you didn't need a job. You were a respectable beggar.

The monastic path remains a great tool for seeing into the situation of human suffering. And actually, I recall that one of my favorite Buddhist teachers, a witty British monk named Ajahn Amaro, once used a surfing metaphor to describe why. He explained how surfers struggle and struggle to get out into the waves. They get three seconds of fun, he said, and get pounded. Then they fight and struggle some more for another measly three seconds. "It's a perfect metaphor for suffering," the Ajahn said.

I agree completely. And the monastic path gives one a chance to stop struggling through work, bills, and finding the perfect mate, only to achieve moments of satisfaction. The problem is that most of us don't want to be monks or nuns. We probably want a romantic relationship, not to mention an occasional good movie, and a nice new surfboard once a year. And that means we have to work.

From a certain linear perspective, where enlightenment is something to *achieve* like a good severance check, all of us normal people are necessarily behind on the path; those bald-headed robed people are beating us up to Enlightenment Peak.

But there's another perspective. The Buddha also said that, from his perspective, samsara already *is* nirvana, that there is no enlightened mind to achieve, no falling behind on the path, and, in fact, no path to begin with. This later became the fundamental point of Zen and resulted in the masters harping away on the fact that you can get enlightened doing anything. As I already mentioned, the guy who went on to become sixth Ancestor of Zen, an illiterate peasant, got enlightened while doing his job: chopping wood. "Before enlightenment, chop wood carry water; after enlightenment, chop wood carry water."

I'd always had a hard time with this teaching, which is probably why I'd gone from being a wannabe monk to a surf bum. But in that moment, huffing and puffing through the stockades at Ocean Beach, I think I got a glimpse. From the perspective of utter love for surfing, paddling was always okay, no matter how difficult, no matter how hopeless. Sure, it wasn't always as fun as riding a wave. But it was part of it. They were the same—interdependent. No paddle, no surf. No samsara, no nirvana.

PADDLING OUT

And if paddling on a day like this could be enjoyable, I figured maybe all of life's challenges could be—maybe even a real job.

Maybe there was no rat race to escape...

5. THE REST OF THE DAY, whenever I had trouble paddling back out through the surf I started chanting: "Samsara is nirvana; samsara is nirvana; samsara is nirvana."

At one point, I started chanting a little too loudly and a guy I was surfing with (not a Buddhist) paddled up to me.

"Dude, what the hell are you yelling about?"

He was the type who might have found Sanskrit chanting a bit spooky. So I tried to find a translation.

"Um, I'm just telling myself over and over again: No pain, no gain. No pain, no gain. It helps me keep paddling."

"Oh, right on. Cause it sounded like some voodoo shit for a minute."

"Yeah. It gets weird out here sometimes."

When I got out of the water, I thought about my life with fresh perspective. Up until this point, I had been drifting. I had been like a jellyfish, floating on the currents, hoping good food would get caught in my tentacles with no effort at all. Granted, that strategy had worked pretty well for a while. And I don't want to knock jellyfish—they're kind of the Taoists of the sea.

But I wasn't a jellyfish. I had flippers, I mean fingers, with opposable thumbs. I had a human body. I could get a job. That's what we humans did.

PADDLING OUT

Yes, I could and *would* get a job, a good job.

And I would gleefully paddle through all the lame parts and ride through the good times with grace and style.

6. WHAT JOB, THOUGH, EXACTLY?

I had become pretty good at surfing and sitting still for long periods. And I had a degree in Religious Studies, the epitome of uselessness. Who would hire me? What was I going to do—write a book about Zen and surfing? Who would read it?

Even the Buddha—the man who formalized homelessness—said that if you're not going to be a monk, you needed a *Right Livelihood*. It was another part of his very first talk, part of the Noble Eightfold Path. Right Livelihood, he said, meant doing something for a living that does not harm others. And I was just mooching off my cousin's generosity.

I thought about graduate school. But in what? I'd had enough of religious scholars for the moment, so a Ph.D. was out of the question. As a kid, I'd wanted to do everything from archaeology to medicine to acting. And everything still *kind of* interested me. But nothing interested me enough to go deep. Every subject was so specialized it seemed like entering an endless digression into tedium that didn't apply to everyday life.

I thought and thought and trawled the Internet and talked to my mom, the career counselor, and that, of course, frustrated me even more. But then it hit me—a real revelation. And it came flooding. And I saw my future unfolding before my eyes. And it was beautiful and perfect: 007, Indiana Jones, *Baywatch*, and *The Insider*, all rolled into one. God, why had I never thought of it before? A job that would let me keep traveling the world and visiting exotic surf breaks, a job that would let me study everything without requiring me to spend my life in a cubicle: *journalism.*

It was so perfect. Journalism was nebulous enough that it could match the needs of my fickle bliss, yet firm enough to make me some cold hard cash. (Now a working journalist, I realize the cold hard cash part of this plan was not pragmatic. But never mind.) I took the appropriate steps—internships and letters of recommendation, and then I took off to Mexico to surf and wait for a response from the journalism schools.

Exactly one year later, while living on rice and beans in a town called Puerto Escondido, Mexico, I got the news: Jaimal Yogis, Buddhist, surf bum, had been accepted to the Columbia University Graduate School of Journalism in *New York City*.

7. ALL RIGHT, it may not sound like such a big deal. But having graduated from one of the lowest ranked academic institutions in the country, I didn't expect to get in anywhere, let alone the *best* ranked graduate school. I half thought there was some mistake. But there was the evidence on my e-mail account. *Accepted.* I was really doing it—finding a Right Livelihood, riding the wave of happiness and prosperity. And in celebration, I immediately Googled "Surf, New York City." (Contrary to popular belief, I'd heard there was surf in New York.)

"New York, New York," I sang quietly as the incredibly slow search engine searched. "New York here I co—Oh man, *really?"*

There was a problem: New York City had exactly one surf spot on the fringes of Brooklyn near Coney Island, about a ninety-minute subway ride from the university. I wouldn't have time for that. Granted, the master's in journalism was only ten months long. But ten months without surf! I took a deep breath. Okay, so it would be a ten-month long paddle. I closed my eyes: *Samsara is Nirvana. Samsara is Nirvana.*

8. I WAS BORN ON LONG ISLAND and ever since I was little I'd wanted to live in New York City. As a boy, I loved bobbing and weaving through the streets dodging hotdog venders and old women with poodles: crowd surfing.

So when I arrived in Manhattan, all that pent-up desire released. I felt like a light bulb in Times Square that would never need changing. Once school started, I didn't sleep. I pulled all-nighters. I wrote award-winning articles (well, one award-winning article). I made friends from all over the world and we stayed up late discussing all kinds of things. I scheduled interviews with city officials and movie stars. (The movie stars never returned my calls, but I was trying.) I practically lived on the subway and ate doughnuts and pizza for dinner. I felt the pulse of America in my veins. For the first time in my life I was totally connected to the mainstream and loving it. It was like living inside MTV. I hardly noticed that I was beginning to twitch involuntarily from too much caffeine, that my muscles were beginning to atrophy, and that none of my belts fit anymore.

No time to note trivialities.

9. BUT EVERY ACTION HAS A REACTION. After a few months of replacing sleep, meditation, and surfing with massive amounts of coffee, the *New Yorker*, and pizza slices the size of a small dog, I felt depressed for the first time in my life. I'd always wondered what people meant when they said the word *depression*. "Just look on the bright side," I wanted to tell those people. "Take up surfing, climb a mountain. Do *something*."

Hearing the word had been like listening to my parents complain of their "stress" when I was little and wondering, "What the hell are they talking about?"

But now, depression was upon me.

At this point in my life, I could tell you who "Brangelina" was, who Britney was dating, which bills were being passed in the senate, and who would most likely win the World Series.

But I suddenly couldn't tell myself why life was worth living. I couldn't find *me* anymore, couldn't remember.

It was like amnesia.

10. AND THEN I GOT SICK: cold after fever after flu. I tried to meditate but it didn't help. I was no longer paddling out. I was drowning.

One cold November night, tucked into my barren Harlem apartment, I broke. I put down my journalism work. I threw out the stacks of magazines and newspapers. I told my roommate, an ultra-disciplined Oxford grad, not to wake me up the next day because I wasn't getting up. And I immersed myself in the only thing in my room that seemed remotely comforting: *Moby Dick*.

"Whenever I find myself growing grim about the mouth," says Ishmael on the first page, "whenever it is a damp, drizzly November in my soul, whenever I find myself involuntarily pausing before coffin warehouses... I account it high time to get to sea as soon as possible."

"Yes, yes, yes," I chanted under the covers. I knew exactly how Ishmael felt. Why had I ever left? Why hadn't I stayed in Mexico, poor and happy? A poem by the Sufi mystic Kabir came to mind: The truth is you turned away yourself and decided to walk into the dark alone. Now... you have forgotten what you once knew.

I had forgotten. And now I was depressed and $52K in debt to boot.

All I knew was that I had to get to the sea.

11. COLUMBIA BARELY GAVE US enough time to shower, let alone go the beach. But that night, I concocted a plan. All of us had to complete a year-long magazine-style feature article, something so riveting it would remain in the grand Columbia library collecting dust for generations to come. And I got an idea: I decided I would report on the growing trend of brazen winter surfers in Montauk, a small fishing town on the eastern-most tip of Long Island.

I would buy a super winter wetsuit and snow surf my way to a master's degree, tricking all these stuffy New Yorkers into letting me have a life. It was perfect.

"It sounds, well, *boring*," my advisor, the former religion writer for the *New York Times*, said to me shockingly, in his navy blue blazer. "I mean they surf, they go home. Where's the news?"

"But in the *snow*," I said. "They surf in the snow! It's incredible."

"I don't think so. But I like your enthusiasm. Keep it up."

12. A FEW DAYS LATER, I came back to him with another idea: "Okay," I said, "How about commercial fishermen in Montauk? I mean, they're a dying breed, right? There are hardly any fish left for them to catch. What are these guys going to do when the fish run out? Someone has to write how they live. You know, their *struggle*." I would make that sacrifice, I told him. I would get aboard a commercial fishing boat and ride it through a harrowing East Coast winter. I would chronicle first-hand the most dangerous job in the world.

"I hope you can get on a boat," he said.

13. January. Cold. *Arctic* cold.

Cold that no Californian should have to endure.

Al, the owner of a local motel, picked me up at the train station in a beat-up pick-up with no heat.

"Welcome to Montauk," he said. "Glad to have you. But what in God's name brought you here in January?"

"Fishing."

"Well, I won't be coming with you. That's for sure."

Al said Montauk went from a population of thirty thousand in the summer to about three thousand in the winter—and most of those rarely left their homes except to buy more whiskey. He was happy to have a single customer and charged me a hundred bucks for the week.

"That's what I charge the deckhands when they come in from a fishing trip, and that's what I'll charge you."

"Thanks, Al. I feel like one of the guys already."

PADDLING OUT

14. THE AIR HOVERED AROUND TWENTY DEGREES with glacial winds out of the north. The sea and sky were the same color, a silvery-grey. The beach was bleak, covered in a foot of snow.

It looked nothing like the California or Hawaii beaches I missed.

And yet, after months away from any aqueous horizon—any broad horizon for that matter—it seemed the most glorious thing I'd ever seen. Tears welled up as I stood watching snowflakes dissolve on the black water and blanket the sand. The wind blew the snow into gentle steps like the inside of a spiral seashell.

I breathed deep, almost for the first time since I'd arrived in New York, and my mind settled, just a bit. I felt a taste of that other kind of contentment that doesn't come from acquiring information or getting praise or building a résumé, the kind that is just there, like a hidden pearl.

The sun set, turning the grey sky orange, the snow pink. Snow fell heavier and heavier, thicker and thicker, whiter and whiter.

"Thank you," I whispered to the sea.

I was finally home, safe and sound.

Or so I thought.

15. THE NEXT MORNING I wandered through the ghost town and stumbled into a tiny Tudor-style church to get warm. A handful of retired captains sat in the pews, discernible by their beards and leathered skin. The reverend led a silk-robed choir in song:

> Mighty tides about me sweep,
> Perils lurk within the deep,
> Angry clouds o'er-shade the sky,
> And the tempest rises high;
> Still I stand the tempest's shock,
> For my anchor grips the rock.
> And it holds, my anchor holds!

The sermon, too, turned out to be about the wrath of the ocean: "'God's voice is over the waters,'" the reverend read from Psalm 29. "'It breaks the cedars, it flashes forth flames of fire and shakes the wilderness'... But is this really the God you want to encounter on your walks on the trails or out on the boat?" One of the retired fishermen seated in the pews shut his eyes and shook his head, presumably recalling storms past.

Later, I walked down to the docks to ask the captains about taking me fishing. I was cheery, enthusiastic. "Hi there! I'm a journalism student trying to learn about commercial fishing," I said, smiling. "I'd like to come with you on a fishing trip."

The captains, dressed in flannels or thin sweaters, looked at me—a multi-colored marshmallow in two pairs of pants, a down jacket, gloves, a wool scarf, and a knit cap—like I was a different species. "Too much responsibility," they glowered. "You'll go green. You'll fall overboard. You'll get in the way."

I could handle it, I told the captains. I was used to the rough ocean. I was a *surfer*.

"Yeah, well, this ain't surfin'," the captains each said, as if they were all the same person. "This is fishin'—winter fishin'."

16. THIS WAS NOT ENCOURAGING. I spent a couple days regrouping; I took long walks on the beach, meditated in my hotel room, made one disastrously cold surfing attempt, and read Steinbeck novels, none of which got me any closer to getting on a fishing boat or writing a master's thesis. "Stay focused," I thought, "Samsara is nirvana." I needed to get on a fishing boat.

But how? The captains were all annoyed with me by this point and a few of them thought I was an undercover agent for the Department of Environmental Conservation trying to bust them for overfishing. Then I had another idea, perhaps the best one yet: I would get the captains *drunk*.

Strictly speaking, this wasn't a very Buddhist thing to do. But I was desperate, and if drinking was what people did in winter Montauk, I figured I needed to go with the flow, conform to the Tao of Montauk.

At any rate, there were about six bars open in the wintertime and the locals all told me that which one you go to depends on just how local you are. I decided I would visit a different pub each night, working my way up the ladder of localness, buying drink after drink for the fishermen.

17. LIAR'S SALOON WAS MY LAST HOPE and I'd been avoiding it. It was a fishermen-only hangout, I'd been told. Even a lot of the longtime locals told me they stayed away because it was too rowdy.

When I told a cabbie that I wanted a ride to Liar's, she looked at me earnestly and said, "You sure about that? You look like such a nice kid." And then she laughed.

Liar's was a shack on a dock lit up against the dark water. A sign at the bar said:

MONTAUK
A QUAINT DRINKING VILLAGE
WITH A FISHING PROBLEM

18. INSIDE, about ten fishermen were gambling and throwing back shots. More were filtering in by the minute. When an old-timer walked in the room, the rookies would literally compete for who could buy all his drinks. The golden bell that hung above the bar, a signal that some fisherman had bought the whole bar a round, went off every five minutes. Apparently, I wouldn't get to do much of the buying here.

Ronnie, a captain who I'd met on the docks a few weeks before, walked in with his crew, smelling—perhaps unsurprisingly—like fish. Apparently, he had just come back with 60,000 pounds of fish, a very big catch. "So you're still at it?" he asked me, winking out of his LIAR'S hoodie. I nodded and asked him how his trip was. "We're feeding the world," he shouted over the music, and he patted me on the shoulder—firmly. I almost fell over.

Ronnie's crew was laughing through their scruffy beards, buying each other round after round of whiskey and Bud. They had twenty-four hours to party before their boat, *Tenacious*, shipped out for another week.

Weather reports said a snowstorm with ten-foot seas was coming in fast—the next voyage would be rough. "We don't care," said Ronnie when I asked him about it, throwing back a gulp of whiskey. "The stormier it is, the more money I make. The harder it blows, the more I can pay my guys."

Did I really want to get on a boat with them? I was still terrified. But it's strange how life works. I'm not big on promulgating universal principles, but this seems to be one: confront your fears and they transform.

I pressed on.

19. AND IT JUST SORT OF HAPPENED.

Within five minutes at Liar's everyone was treating me like I was somehow one of them, telling me stories about their wives and kids. It was actually the most welcoming bar I've ever been to.

I started talking with a captain named Mike, a young guy with a thick Jersey accent, who, for no apparent reason, seemed determined to tell me his life story from beginning to end. It was interesting, too. And I kept buying him beer. About an hour went by, and after who knows how many beers between us— and just as Mike was getting around to his high school years—he said the magic words: "So, you want to go fishing? I'll take you fishing. But you get buried, it's not my problem."

20. MIKE WAS STRONG AND STOCKY with a full beard and rectangular glasses. He wore dirty, baggy jeans and a MONTAUK hoodie with a knit cap, at least when he was working, which was almost always. In high school, Mike was a Deadhead, trying to make it to every Grateful Dead show he could. The funny thing is that Montauk residents call fishermen "fishheads." Mike was a Deadhead-fishhead: something he seemed very proud of.

He was captain of the *Virginia Victoria*, a small boat his dad had helped him buy. We were scheduled to leave on Saturday. But when Saturday came it was too rough for the small boat, so we postponed until Sunday night when the storm had subsided.

I was excited—and again, terrified. Mike had gotten a survival suit for me, but going overboard wasn't what I feared. I kept remembering the warnings I'd gotten from an Irish fisherman about seasickness: "You're going to go green your first trip," he'd said. "It's the worst thing imaginable. There is no escape."

21. I ARRIVED AT THE DOCK pumped full of Dramamine. A man named Tiernan, who looked like a fatter, roughed-up George Clooney, welcomed me aboard with a raspy voice. "Call me T.," he said.

"No 'Mister'?" I asked, trying to be funny.

"No," he said without even a hint of a smile. "Just T."

It was going to be an interesting trip.

The *Virginia* glowed underneath the electric dock lights. She was an older boat with rusted gear and a torn-up green net. The cabin was coated in chipped white paint. The hull was deep forest green.

The kitchen was a mass of paper cups, newspapers, cigarette packs, water jugs, and, for some reason, old pieces of toast. It smelled like pepperoni pizza and sardines. Fishhooks and bait dangled from the ceiling like Christmas ornaments. The beds, about the size of coffins, were in a small chamber down below.

But we wouldn't really be using the beds. As it turned out, fishermen, like Zen monks, hardly sleep. We steamed out of the harbor under the stars at 3:00 AM. It was bumpy: six-foot waves every eight seconds, and before long, the *Virginia* was bobbing up and down like an apple. On the downward cadence, the bow dipped and white spume covered the windows.

But setting off into pitch-black night and open ocean, no sound but the grind of the engine, was somehow serene. Steinbeck wrote on going to sea that

"The matters of great importance we had left were unimportant... We had lost the virus, or it had been eaten by antibodies of quiet."

As the *Virginia* careened off the waves, I didn't ask Mike any journalistic questions. The antibodies of quiet did their work.

It was everything I'd romantically imagined.

It was kind of like paddling out at Ocean Beach, but with a motor and a heater: easy. I wasn't sick or cold.

And those captains had thought I couldn't hang. I was *fine*.

But, as the Buddha taught all those centuries ago: everything changes.

22. AN HOUR IN, I was sweating. Ninety minutes, and I was horribly dizzy. Something in my intestines was beginning to grow and writhe like an eel. Five more minutes and I felt like one of the infected crewmembers in Alien. The eel was angry. I tried to fight it. But there was no escape. I was going green. I ran out on the deck.

"Don't puke over the sides!" Mike yelled. There were no railings on the *Virginia*. Even a small wave could send me overboard if I were leaning over the edge. The waves were already bigger and buckets and fish bins were smashing against the walls of the boat. I could barely stand.

I vomited out salty almonds onto the deck as a big wave crashed over the railing. The wind felt like needle-size icicles on my skin. The cold killed some of the nausea, but I was soon shivering even with three layers and a down coat (no one had told me that down loses its insulating quality when wet!). I tried to stumble into the cabin to get warm but each time I entered I would rush out again to vomit. I was also exhausted from not sleeping. Occasionally, I nodded off against a grey fish bin. But when I did, a wave would knock me and everything else on deck to the opposite side of the boat. I would hit the wall, fall to my knees, hurl again, drink a little water, fall over, hurl once more.

For hours.

By the time we stopped to drop the net, I was lying on the deck and dry-heaving like a dying horse.

"Rise and shine, Mister Journalist," Mike chuckled. "We're here."

"Home?"

"The middle of the ocean."

"Can we go home?"

"We haven't even started fishin'. Hey, you're the one who wanted to come out here."

Daybreak had finally come and there was nothing around but grey clouds and black water. Tiernan waddled out onto the deck in his plastic orange overalls. The boat rocked and swayed at forty-five-degree angles, but 250-pound T. moved with it, never losing his balance. "So you wanted to know what commercial fishing in the winter is like," he yelled over the waves. "Now you know. I told you, we're not right in the head."

I thought it was possibly the worst day of my life.

"Hey, it beats working a nine-to-five," T. said.

23. I WAS ALMOST DELIRIOUS, but watching T. work, I saw something about life and work and the nature of the struggle. It was all relative. Against the backdrop of commercial fishing, journalism seemed suddenly like the best job in the world (provided you weren't covering commercial fishing). Finishing my master's seemed like a pleasant weekend stroll.

I realized I needed to stop complaining. I had it very, very easy.

If I come out of this alive, I said to myself, I will have *perspective*.

24. For the next hour, I lay on a bench under the dining room table, trying to focus on impermanence, mainly the fact that this would all (eventually) be over. Then Mike's radio sounded. "We're getting our asses whooped out here, man," a voice said. "The storm is coming in." The message was from a bigger boat offshore.

Oh, please, I thought. No more storms. Send sea monsters, a plague of locusts, a rain of fire. But no more waves.

Mike came out and said we were going to turn around after they pulled the fish up. "Sometimes we play it safe," he said. "The weather's comin' in."

Really, I think Mike took pity on me.

He later said that on a scale of one to ten, that day was about a five. But every fisherman knows what it's like to be sick. "You just stick your finger down your throat and keep working," Mike said. "It sucks. But, hey, people gotta eat. And we gotta eat."

The net brought in about 250 pounds of fish, mostly skates, which look like little stingrays. They lay there on the deck gasping helplessly at the oxygen they couldn't breathe. The skates would fetch them about ten cents per pound at the market, where people bought them for bait. There were also a few monkfish, ugly bottom-feeders with double jaws, and some flounder, which Mike kept live to sell to Chinese markets. There were at least twenty dogfish, shark-looking grey things that have no market value whatsoever. They were cut up in the net, dripping blood onto the deck.

Mike and T. spent the next hour picking out the keepers while the Grateful Dead's *American Beauty* blasted over the roar of the waves.

I managed to shoot some photos in between heaves. "What a trooper," Mike said at one point. "Puking and taking photos. Good journalist."

And that was the closest I would get to being a Montauk local, or a sailor, or a commercial fisherman.

25. Six hours later, back at my motel, I slept for thirteen hours and dreamt of swaying ships, war, and flopping grey fish that ate human fingers. I woke up feeling hungover. It had snowed a few inches overnight and I stumbled down to the beach. The frothy white sea-foam was kissing the snowline on the sand with each surge.

Walt Whitman once visited Montauk and wrote a poem:

> I stand as on some mighty eagle's beak,
> Eastward the sea absorbing, viewing,
>   (nothing but sea and sky),
> The tossing waves, the foam, the ships in
>   the distance,
> The wild unrest, the snowy, curling
>   caps—that inbound urge and urge of
>   waves,
> Seeking the shores forever.

I'd come to Montauk thinking it was my destiny to seek the shores forever. But now I was wondering if maybe I had to give my Zen dolphin-boy fantasies a rest.

Maybe I should just that let whole thing go.

Maybe.

Part IX
NOT DEAD YET

When we finally know we are dying, and all other sentient beings are dying with us, we start to have a burning, almost heartbreaking sense of the fragility and preciousness of each moment and each being.
—Sogyal Rinpoche

I'm not afraid of death…
I just don't want to be there when it happens.
—Woody Allen

In the beginner's mind, there are many possibilities. In the expert's mind, there are few.
—Shunryu Suzuki

1. RIDING THE SUBWAY in February with a surfboard drew plenty of attention.

"Hawaii-bound, eh?" a businessman asked.

"Nope. Brooklyn." I was headed to that surf break I'd found out about on the Internet. Favorable conditions had finally aligned themselves with my free time, and I was not going to let the opportunity pass.

The businessman looked confused and turned away.

Headed through Williamsburg, a group of junior high students spotted me.

"Are you carrying an *ironing* board?" a boy with dreadlocks asked.

"No, this is a surfboard."

"A surfboard—you crazy?"

"Yes, actually."

"It's snowman season."

"I know."

"That's crazy."

"I know."

"*Shit.*"

"I know."

2. I WALKED OUT INTO THE SNOW. It was falling steadily in heavy white flakes, in sheets. The snow on the sidewalk was up to my knees and I trudged toward what I hoped was the beach: past a pizza parlor, past some dilapidated apartment buildings, past a crew of guys drinking out of brown paper bags around a garbage fire.

I ducked into a liquor store and asked where the beach was.

"Why you wanna know?" the clerk asked. (I'd left my board outside.)

"Just want to see the beach in the snow. I'm from California. Homesick, I guess."

"It's nothin' special. That's for sure. It's that way. Just keep walkin.'"

"Thanks."

"Hope you brought your bathin' suit."

"Oh, I did."

It was thirty degrees and already seemed to be getting dark at three in the afternoon.

I found the beach.

I think that if ghettos in Siberia had beaches, they would look something like the 98th Street beach did that day. There were chain-linked fences and boarded up apartments and broken down cars all along the road parallel with the coast. Everything was covered in white. It was hard to even see the waves through the snow. But from the walkway that lined the beach,

3. MY LITHUANIAN GREAT-GRANDPARENTS settled in Brooklyn in the early twentieth century. I wondered what they would have said if they knew their great-grandson would be *surfing* there one hundred years later in mid-winter. "Not our grandson," they would've probably said (once someone explained what surfing was). "He's going to be a smart one."

I changed into my suit on the boardwalk, shrieking as my bare feet touched the snow before slipping them into my booties. "Praise the booties. Praise the booties," I mumbled, rushing to put on the rest: a thick hood and lobster gloves.

With zippers up and elastic cinched tight as it could go, I sprinted into the water before I could hesitate.

7. As I GOT CLOSER, I saw that there were a few other nut cases in the water, too. So at least I wasn't alone. (If you're an addict, it seems somehow different when you're around other addicts.) I watched one of them catch a perfect left and I forgot all about being crazy. I forgot about the long ride and the cold water. I remembered why I'd come.

And before long, I was on one of those lefts, the first *real* wave I'd caught all year. It was a few feet overhead, and thick, and long. I rode it unexpectedly well, flipping two backside snaps off the lip, then staying high on the inclining wall to maintain speed, through the fast pitching section, and ending with a mini-floater across the cold suds. It was a *good* wave, as good as almost any point wave I'd ridden in California—but strangely, surreally, this one was in Brooklyn, in the snow. I caught wave after wave and chatted with the two other surfers who lived in Brooklyn and surfed the break all the time. They said I'd lucked out, that it didn't get like this all that often.

I was having so much fun. But the waves were coming in close together and I was out of shape; after an hour I was having an impossible time paddling back. I noticed one of the guys was walking out to the take-off point on the jetty, skipping the paddle-out. He had to time the sets and jump in at the right moment so he wouldn't get smashed. But it looked easy enough. I followed, jumping across the riprap with my shiny new board.

I made the entry easily. Rode a good wave in. And decided to do it again.

But by the time I'd made it to the beach, the sun was setting and the other guys were getting out. They waved and I considered going in. Nah. One more wave, I told myself, just one, then back on the subway, back to Manhattan, back to work.

I hurried across the stones, avoiding the ice patches, and as I walked I remember admiring how I hadn't lost my skills after almost eight months without waves. I was a *surfer*. And there wasn't any better thing to be in the wor—

"*Oh my God!*"

5. I SUDDENLY WAS STARING at a beautiful emerald green wall of water spackled with white foam, towering above me. It had come from nowhere: a sleeper— a rogue. There was nothing I could do. Sharp rocks were on all sides of me and I was in the wave's shadow. And it was falling—fast. I leapt into it, board out in front of me, as it hollowed and fell. But I couldn't pierce it. It was thick, its lip alone several feet wide. The wall slapped me backward easily, like a grizzly batting a river salmon.

It all happened quickly. But time moved slower as I flew back, back, back—suspended, it seemed, for seconds, an eternity. I shut my eyes, and as I fell, I had one thought: *this is it.*

I was sure the wave would smack me against the riprap and crack my skull or shatter my spinal column into thousands of pieces. Scientists would find me many years from now floating in an iceberg, my leash still clinging to my ankle. They would remark, no doubt dispassionately, how dumb I must have been to be surfing in mid-winter in the first place.

And then I hit. *Fwap-swashle-blup-slup-shwop-fwaboosh!* My body bounced. But not hard like I'd expected. Something—the water?—wrapped around my body: a soft cloak. And then all was dark. And quiet. And I was deep below.

Maybe this is death, I thought. The quiet before... whatever. And in the cold dark, I was surprisingly unafraid. I couldn't breathe for some immeasurable amount of time. It felt like the sea was just sitting on me, waiting, pondering. And under her weight, momentarily, everything went soft like a scribbly television screen with a faint buzz, like a field of dry grass, like a leaf.

But then I needed air. I really needed air. And I gulped and struggled. And finally, it lifted. And I was rising, then choking, then gasping, then breathing. And I wasn't dead. I wasn't dea—

"Oh motherf—!"

Another wave, equally thick, equally powerful, surged onto me. It lifted me up, then shoved me down, back into that graveyard of riprap. Bones jangled against sharp corners. Arms covered head. Body curled into a ball. Chaos. Swirling. Dark again. Pressure. I felt to my left (rock), to my right (rock), above me (rock). I was wedged *under boulders under water*. But still, apparently, not dead. *Not dead*, the thought repeated. *Not dead*.

My body wiggled and pried. And loose from whatever I'd been wedged into, I swam—up, up, up— toward the light.

And that's when I noticed the speck. Bright. A very bright speck, a grey laser point of light. And then the laser point opened. And it was a... was it a bird? It was so bright, but bigger now. No, it was a cloud. Yes, it was turning into a cloud. And I was breathing again. No, it was several clouds. Lots of clouds. And then it opened fully, as if the whole view had been constructed from that single point of light. And I saw it clearly. The sky. Of course. The sky, so bright grey. So blinding.

I looked down and saw the water. Black. Metallic black. *Bright black*. There was the sea and the sky and there was bright light everywhere. Light all around me. Nothing but light.

And the light came together—cohered into shapes. Sky. Sea. Cloud. I breathed. And it was loud—the breath. And the crackling sea. The water droplets popped like, like, *Rice Krispies*. It was all so loud and bright and hard—very hard.

Down there it's quiet, came the thought. *Dark. Soft. No edges. No sharp lines.*

Down there.

6. I FELT MY BODY. Covered in this weird thick rubber. Bruised. Definitely bruised. But *functioning*. Limbs all there. *Human limbs.* My board was gone, shattered fiberglass, gone forever.

And that's when I realized I was floating next to the jetty. Next to the rocks. Sharp rocks. Senses sharpened. Hearing. Sight. *Danger.* The waves had stopped briefly. I was between sets. I could see the horizon. She, the sea, was letting me go. And then, everything popped: Yes. She was letting me go. Light. Clarity. Life. I wanted it. I definitely wanted it.

And so I swam. I swam hard, away from the jetty, out beyond the breaking waves. And I floated there for a moment in the deep black water and looked around at the inhuman vastness and felt like a minute piece of sand. I swam toward shore, coughing up saltwater as I pulled. I swam and swam and crawled out of the water, laying belly down against the snow. I placed my bare cheek on the cold whiteness. It burned. I licked it. *Pure water.* Sweet water.

I took a bite.

7. I FLIPPED ONTO MY BACK. It was snowing lightly now, gently. My breathing was heavy, with a grinding sound in my chest. I was delirious, definitely not *right* somehow. Yet also clear, more clear than usual, I thought. I ran through what I knew.

I knew who I was. Jaimal Nikos Yogis.

I hadn't lost it all. I could feel the weight of my body on the snow. Solid. I knew that I was in Brooklyn and that I had to go back to class soon. Yes, class.

But I also was seeing differently, seeing—how should I say—as if in surround-sound, not just through the eyes. More of a *tactile* seeing, above and below and to the sides seeing. And I don't really know how to put this in words, but I saw all the *stuff* of my life—stories, and careers, and buddhas, and surfboards, and girlfriends—as if from a distance, and it seemed somehow unreal, like a bad sitcom. I didn't want to pick it all up. *Not yet*, I thought. *Just wait... just wait a moment.*

Because *the snow. Yes. The snow.* I wanted to watch the snow fall. Just see it. Breathe it. How the flakes drifted down in a pattern. Yes, I was almost sure of it. And I'd never noticed it in such a way. But it was—it was a pattern of falling, too complex to decipher, and always changing. But perfectly ordered. Every flake, placed just so, fluttering just right. And each one so delicate, so intricate, so different. And so fundamentally the same. I cried just because. And it felt wonderful. It felt like an immeasurable burden was lifting from my chest. I let my tears fall into the snow.

I cried for a minute, or two, or five. I don't know. But then I sat up and looked around. Big sea. White beach. Beige apartments.

And now it seemed okay to pick it all up. *Me*. To pick *that* up too.

Something—I wasn't quite sure what—seemed funny, humorous. I chuckled. Maybe it was that I was sitting in the snow in Brooklyn with a leash attached to my ankle and I couldn't really think of a good reason why. Maybe it was that I was alive. Maybe I shouldn't have been. But I was, indeed, *alive*. And that was curiously funny. Yes. That was it. Even the word seemed odd and fresh. *A-l-i-v-e*.

How? How was I alive? How was I assimilating it all at once, all this form, sensation, memory, perception, consciousness? They were coalescing into this, this *thing* I looked through, like a box with a few holes in it. How had all this stardust and gas and dark matter and comets *burst* and made *this* pattern? A pattern like a snowflake. So freakishly unique, and yet so much like every other.

A human pattern—a story that tried desperately to make sense. But ultimately, just fell and fell and fell, like snowflakes, like wave after wave. This pattern's only job was to be, perfectly, just where it was.

And then to melt.
Flow. Wind. Crash. Rush.
And then to become, finally, the sea.

Part X
ONE MORE WAVE

Who need be afraid of the merge?
—Walt Whitman

The path was narrow and my clothes kept catching,
The moss so spongy I couldn't move my feet.
So I stopped under this red cinnamon tree.
I guess I'll lay my head on a cloud and sleep.
—Han-Shan

1. FOG HOVERING LOW. So low, it looks as if the sea is vaporizing. Sun sending the final rays through the opaque curtain. A seagull flies overhead, its white feathers hardly distinguishable from the clouds.

Zen Master Hung-chih wrote on the day of his death:

> Illusory dreams, phantom flowers—
> Sixty-seven years
> A white bird vanishes in the mist,
> Autumn waters merge with the sky

The bird apparently refers to the ego, finally merging with the One, or the Tao, or something. But the lines ring more literally out in the fog, where everything seems almost soluble, disappearing, reappearing.

These days, I'm not doing any dissolving. I feel my body distinctly, aching in all sorts of ways. It's the fifth in a string of good big surf days, which I have spent getting pummeled, flung about like a piece of dust in a hurricane, only occasionally feeling any—let alone much—control. I am so physically exhausted that my body seems more interested in drifting now than catching waves, simply grateful for a board to lay on, for the thickness of seawater, for buoyancy.

It's a good fatigue. No distinct hunger for waves, but a satisfaction in being among them.

ONE MORE WAVE

The fog is blocking the wind, making the ocean smooth as silk, as swamp water. But it's blocking my vision, too. I can just barely make out the color or shape of the waves until they're right in front of me.

It's a bit unsettling. Looking back toward the beach, I might as well be lost at sea: nothing but white in front, nothing but white behind, to the sides—white. And it's the same bubble vision no matter which direction I paddle. Completely unknown.

But when I accept the fact that I can't mark my place, can't predict where I'm floating to, it becomes fun in a different way: completely intuitive.

Nowhere to paddle to. Nowhere for the currents to drag me from.

"Oh," I can't help thinking, "finally, I'm actually doing it—Zen surfing."

2. THIS IS SAN FRANCISCO, by the way, down the street from where my girlfriend and I live on the top floor of a big house on La Playa Street, right on Ocean Beach. (The houseboat didn't work out.) It's been about two and a half years since I left New York. I escaped 98th Street with only a few bad bruises. And I graduated. Having never had a high school or college graduation ceremony (I was always moving too much), the ten-month paddle was well worth the party wave. Friends flew in. Relatives wrote checks. Bartenders poured free drinks. Dancing happened by itself.

And now I do in fact have a real job. I write for *San Francisco Magazine* and it's really not bad. It's not killing me or making me depressed like graduate school (thank God that's over). I have time to surf and do my little zazen sessions just about everyday. I make just enough money (if I keep a steady diet of burritos) to live in this small apartment with a slight ocean view.

I don't always like my job.

In fact, I'm sort of dreading this upcoming article I volunteered to do on Nancy Pelosi, which mean going to DC and probably missing good waves and pretending I know what the Speaker of the House does. But I can't complain. My editor has already let me write a long story about surfing in San Francisco, as well as one on my friend's garage band.

And when I asked him if I could have six months off from my writing contract to work on a book about Zen and surfing—if you can imagine—he said, "Sure, go for it."

And, really, how often do you have a boss who would say that?

Everyone who knew me in my running-away-to-Hawaii-every-other-year days is surprised, including me.

Jaimal has a job and he's stayed in the same city for more than a year. He's in a stable healthy relationship with the same girl he's been with for about four years. And for now, they are happy with their simple existence, not looking for much more than this.

Hard to believe.

3. I DON'T KNOW VERY MANY SURFERS in San Francisco. So I usually surf alone, except when my neighbor Noah is around. But that's fine. I'm not striving for the ideal surfer's paradise anymore, or the perfect life without obstacles. It doesn't exist. Not that I don't have preferences or dreams anymore. But it seems like the idea of paradise is just on the horizon, always, while life is *here*, under my feet, now.

Might as well enjoy it, learn to appreciate the good waves, the paddling, the ferocious storms, and the mundane moments—the quiet lulls between swells. Emptiness here, emptiness there, says one famous Zen poem, but the infinite universe stands always before your eyes; infinitely large and infinitely small.

4. IT SEEMS ANY TIME one looks for perfection, or happiness in conditions, it turns to disappointment. I originally wanted to write this whole memoir or whatever you call it on *Dulce*, the sailboat in Sausalito. That was my original plan. I thought that would be romantic and somehow Zen-like to be writing on a boat. But after a couple months, the holding tank, no matter how many times I emptied it, reeked of sewage. And the little bed, the one tucked into the bow, the one I compared to "being in the womb," was right next to the holding tank; so, obviously, it no longer lulled me to sleep. It just smelled like shit.

I guess even the prettiest things eventually end up stinking. Everything does. We all will die and rot and decay and be reborn as dirt or flowers or worms, or polar bears who will drown because their ice is all melting, or presidents of war-torn countries, or whales swimming around acidifying seas. And then we will rot and decay again. And so it goes.

But here's the thing I learned through all this:

I am not what I *think* I am.

I just am.

On the way back from the beach, on the subway that evening in Brooklyn, I was in an altered state. And I saw all the thoughts I thought made "*me*" laid out like a filmstrip. I saw Mom, Pa, Ciel, the Azores, grandparents, metal Buddha statues, friends, Zen masters, France, Hawaii, and surf magazines. I saw that, at best, it was kind of a B-grade film: touching at moments, hilarious at others, a couple steamy scenes tossed in for the audience, but generally monotonous (especially with all the meditation).

And over the next few months, I thought about my life a lot. I thought about how the very things I was searching for freedom in—Buddhas and waves and writing and girlfriends—were probably also partly replacements, symbols, for the lost embrace of my parents, the lost freedom of being held. I even paid a lot of money and talked to psychologists about it and it was interesting. I felt like I was making some progress. And I guess I was; I was changing the film, reorganizing it. Cutting sections, adding new perspectives.

And I thought that I might have wrestled free of the shackles of my history. Maybe life begins now, I thought. I could go to Hollywood. I could be a real writer and go back to New York and do what real writers do: drink expensive scotch and write about sex and death. I could be anybody.

But who? And why? And where?

And how?

5. I FELT LOST AGAIN, exactly the feeling graduate school was supposed to "fix." But then I had a dream. You would think I'd be wary of following my dreams by now. And I am. I don't go flying off to Hawaii every time I have a dream about a palm tree anymore. But this dream was different. It had an entirely different feeling about it. It was just clear and solid and regular. Well, the content wasn't regular, and frankly isn't worth describing. But the point was it didn't *feel* like a dream at all.

And when I woke up, for a moment I wasn't sure if my waking life was actually a dream and my dream was reality. I thought of the old Taoist poet Chuang Tzu who once wrote he didn't know if he was a butterfly dreaming he was man or a man dreaming he was a butterfly. And that reminded me that it's not worth getting all stressed out about being lost or undecided. Lost is just a dream. Undecided is just a perception—a mirage in life's vast desert.

So I relaxed. Things will work out, I thought. They always do. Just take one step forward, Jaimal, just one. The obvious step is there in front of you.

And the next week, I flew home—to California.

6. AND I DON'T WANT to romanticize or spiritualize a dream too much. But everything sort of fell into place after that. Well, as much as things in this life ever can, and for the time-being.

I guess you could say I found *my* middle way. I got my little job and my little house near the beach. And I'm finally in the same city as my girlfriend. We cook and take walks, and I go to that same little monastery in Berkeley to see my old teachers. And they are all the same wonderful people they were when I was eighteen. And they give me good advice and encourage me to keep going with my practice, and with this silly book.

I guess what I'm trying to say is that I'm learning to not want to be someone else, to just be who I am, as is, with nothing extra added on.

I've learned that I'm not the things I do or don't do; I'm not surfing or Buddhism or writing. And yet all those things *are*. And I *am*. And we have naturally run into each other like colliding atoms creating molecules as we sail on into the foggy mystery. As an ancient Zen master said, "Elements of the Self come and go like clouds without purpose." And it all goes more smoothly, I've come to see, if you just let those clouds come and go freely—accept yourself, accept *this*.

That's it; that's my insight as best I can express it with this fumbling language.

ONE MORE WAVE

And like so many of my insights, it hit me while I was out there floating—an empty vessel—on the fingertips of the wide-open sea, my teacher.

Acknowledgments

As I say in the book, I haven't had one teacher I consider a real "guru guru," but I have had many spiritual teachers to whom I am forever indebted. Special thanks to Steven Tainer, who teaches the Dharma more eloquently and truly than anyone I've ever encountered. To Reverend Heng Sure, Doug Powers, Martin Verhoeven, the great master Hsuan Hua, and the entire City of Ten Thousand Buddhas sangha: your compassion and tough love are immeasurable (and yes, I still sit in full lotus). To Thich Nhat Hanh and His Holiness the Dalai Lama for catching me in their vast bodhisattva nets. To Sonam Wangdue, whose smile alone continues to inspire me and give me faith. To Baba Hari Dass, whose light is like a magnet to the Path. To Ajahn Amaro and Ajahn Passano, the wittiest and wisest of the Forest Tradition. To Professor Robert Thurman, for making fun of us Zen heads in constructive ways. To Wes Nisker, Robert Hall, Jack Kornfield, and Spirit Rock (where would the West be without you?). To Stephan Bodian and Karen Sella, who helped me finally integrate what I'd learned. To Mom and Pa, who taught me to find truth within. And to all my friends who have suffered through Chan retreats with me or combed the world's beaches for waves. I'll leave someone out if I name names, but you are *all* my teachers.

This book would not have been possible without the steady perseverance of Josh Bartok, Laura Cunningham, Joe Evans, Rod Meade Sperry, and the rest of the Wisdom crew. I am also extremely grateful to *Shambhala Sun*, the *Utne Reader*, Beliefnet, and TheWorstHorse.net for giving me the necessary momentum to begin and for encouragement and support from Margaret Gee, Michael Ellsberg, Max Track, Phillip Cryan, Gene Schultz, Aran Watson, Ciel Yogis, Noah Borerro, Vineet Jindal, Daniel Duane, Alexandra Rothenberg, Veronica Bollow, my entire family, and the Scull-Weaver family, especially Siri, who is not only a great editor but puts up with living with a surfer. Philip Pascuzzo's superb cover art speaks for itself.

Thomas Farber, Ari Goldman, LynNell Hancock, Judith Matloff, Nina Martin, Nan Wiener, Bruce Kelley, Douglas Mikkelson, and many others helped me immensely with the skills and confidence to pull off a book. Thank you.

About the Author

Jaimal Yogis is an award-winning journalist and photographer who spends a good deal of his spare time surfing and traveling the globe. He has a master's degree in journalism from Columbia University in New York City and his work has been published in *The Washington Post*, *The Chicago Tribune*, *The Toronto Star*, Beliefnet, *Tricycle*, and many other places. He lives in San Francisco and is a regular contributor for *San Francisco Magazine*. Jaimal can be found online at www.jaimalyogis.com

ABOUT WISDOM PUBLICATIONS

WISDOM PUBLICATIONS, a nonprofit publisher, is dedicated to making available authentic works relating to Buddhism for the benefit of all. We publish books by ancient and modern masters in all traditions of Buddhism, translations of important texts, and original scholarship. Additionally, we offer books that explore East-West themes unfolding as traditional Buddhism encounters our modern culture in all its aspects. Our titles are published with the appreciation of Buddhism as a living philosophy, and with the special commitment to preserve and transmit important works from Buddhism's many traditions.

To learn more about Wisdom, or to browse books online, visit our website at www.wisdompubs.org.

You may request a copy of our catalog online or by writing to this address:

Wisdom Publications
199 Elm Street
Somerville, Massachusetts 02144 USA
Telephone: 617-776-7416
Fax: 617-776-7841
Email: info@wisdompubs.org
www.wisdompubs.org

The Wisdom Trust

As a nonprofit publisher, Wisdom is dedicated to the publication of Dharma books for the benefit of all sentient beings and dependent upon the kindness and generosity of sponsors in order to do so. If you would like to make a donation to Wisdom, you may do so through our website or our Somerville office. If you would like to help sponsor the publication of a book, please write or email us at the address above.

Thank you.

Wisdom is a nonprofit, charitable 501(c)(3) organization affiliated with the Foundation for the Preservation of the Mahayana Tradition (FPMT).

Additional Titles from Wisdom Pubications

Hardcore Zen
Punk Rock, Monster Movies, and the Truth About Reality
Brad Warner
224 pages | ISBN 086171380X | $14.95

"Full of sly irreverence, snappy references to contemporary culture, and amusing tangents, Warner brings messages of substance on many introductory Buddhist topics: Zen retreat, meditation, the precepts, reincarnation, etc. For my money, *Hardcore Zen* is worth two or three of those Buddhism-for-Young-People books."—*Shambhala Sun*

One City
A Declaration of Interdependence
Ethan Nichtern
192 pages | ISBN 0861715160 | $15.95

"*One City* is destined to be a modern spiritual classic. Ethan has a powerful voice and is at the forefront of the new generation of spiritual revolutionaries."—Noah Levine, author of *Dharma Punx* and *Against the Stream*

Who Ordered This Truckload of Dung?
Inspiring Stories for Welcoming Life's Difficulties
Ajahn Brahm
288 pages | ISBN 0861712781 | $15.95

"Masterly storytelling and Dharma teaching, beautifully and effectively combined. The tales are at times hilarious, at times poignant; often both."—Larry Rosenberg, author of *Breath by Breath*

Zen Meditation in Plain English
John Daishin Buksbazen | foreword by Peter Matthiessen
128 pages | ISBN 0861713168 | $12.95

"John Daishin Buksbazen has brought the practice of Zen home to us all. It is as simple as stretching exercises, as intimate as counting the breaths, as uncomplicated as accepting one's self, as ordinary as enjoying one's friends."—Robert Aitken, author of *Gateless Gate*